People at Work

THE STUDENT'S BOOK

Edgar Sather, Catherine Sadow
and George Draper

with photographs by Michael Jerald

PRO LINGUA **ASSOCIATES**

Publishers

Published by Pro Lingua Associates
15 Elm Street
Brattleboro, Vermont 05301

802-257-7779
San 216 0579

*At Pro Lingua, our objective is to foster
an approach to learning and teaching which
we call **Interplay**, the **inter**action of language
learners and teachers with their materials,
with the language and the culture, and
with each other in active, creative
and productive **play**.*

People at Work is an adaption of *It's All in a Day's Work* by George Draper and Edgar Sather, which was published and copyrighted © in 1977 by Newbury House Publishers, Inc., of Rowley, Massachusetts, and revised in 1980. The authors and the publisher are grateful to Newbury House for permission to develop and publish this adaptation.

The authors and publisher are also grateful to Douglas William Clegg and to ASCAP for permission to use lyrics and Mr. Clegg's recordings of the three songs used in Lesson 5: *Fill My Thirst, California,* and *You Get What's Coming.* Copyright © 1988 by Douglas William Clegg. All rights reserved.

To purchase Mr. Clegg's recordings or to arrange for personal appearances, write D. W. Clegg, 328 Concord Stage Road, Weare, New Hampshire 03281, or call 603-529-1051.

Permission to use the following readings is gratefully acknowledged: The Institute for Research for "A Career in Banking," pp. 9-11, and "Industrial Engineers Talk," pp. 71-72; Capra Press for "Waitress," pp. 30-31; The Boston Globe for "Volunteers Needed Now," p. 56, and "Guiding Spirit," p. 59; L.L. Bean for their "help wanted" advertisement, p. 67; Northeastern University for the admissions brochure for its engineering school, p. 70; Bantam Books for "Learning to Speak the Native Tongue," p. 73; Sandra Sokoloff and The Boston Globe for "Some colleges work to attract women into engineering," p. 84; and Rebecca Rich and The Washington Post for "My First Stab Wound," p. 94.

The publisher acknowledges the tireless and creative services of Edgar Sather as both interviewer and impresario, contributions to the book far beyond the call of duty as author. Thank you.

ISBN 0-86647-037-9

This student's book is designed to be used with three tapes and an independent study supplement/teacher's book.

People at Work was set in Electra by Stevens Graphics of Brattleboro, Vermont, and printed and bound by Capital City Press of Montpelier, Vermont. It was designed by Arthur A. Burrows.

Printed in the United States of America.   Second Printing, 1994. 7,000 copies in print.

Foreword to the Student

Welcome to People at Work. We hope you enjoy these interviews with people who talk about the work they do and what they enjoy about it. They are interesting and enthusiastic and the stories they tell are often funny. Some of them talk about the unusual paths they've travelled to get to their present positions.

We hope that having your own tapes and being able to listen to the interviews and other listening exercises whenever you wish to will help you enjoy listening to English. You can listen in class, in a language lab, while jogging, or in your kitchen.

This is a listening book with communicative activities or projects for you to do. We feel that listening to the language is very important, but just as we have freed you from listening in class or the lab by giving you tapes, we hope to free you to do some interesting and challenging things with your English: to get out of the classroom, to use your English out in the community, and then to bring what you have learned back into the classroom to share with your classmates. We hope you'll enjoy both the listening and the doing.

Foreword to the Teacher

People at Work, a listening book for intermediate to advanced students, is based on interviews with ten interesting North Americans in the work place.

The book is a revamping of Draper and Sather's *All in a Day's Work*, for which we sought out new workers, totally revised and rerecorded the listening materials, and created all new and different exercises with a strong emphasis on active involvement and the development of communicative skills.

Each lesson is built around first an introduction to and then a recorded interview with a person at work. Following the interview is a recorded idiom and vocabulary exercise in which the students are challenged to deduce — from the context clues provided on the tape — the meaning of key words and phrases in the interview. Next comes a short dialogue which follows up and dramatizes cultural and social issues raised in the interview. An interactive listening activity, designed to build such various skills as note taking, following directions, answering multiple choice questions, and filling out forms, completes the taped material for each lesson.

Central to each lesson are the "experiential activities" which students do individually, or in small groups and which get them out into the community to meet and talk with people. These projects include a variety of activities related to the social and/or cultural issues raised in the interview: researching community resources, polling, interviewing, gathering information for reports. Most of the lessons include a reading related to the interview.

Every student has his or her own tapes, enabling students to work on their own, where and when they want to.

Lesson format

A. Prelistening

Portrait photograph*

Introductory reading*

Work related vocabulary list*

B. The First Listening

The Interview — *on tape*

Questions after the interview, first listening*

Vocabulary in context exercise* — *on tape*

C. The Second Listening

The Interview again — *on tape*

Questions after the interview, second listening

Reconstruction exercise*

D. The Dialogue

Photographs of the workplace*

The Dialogue — *on tape*

Questions after the dialogue*

Interactive listening exercise* — *on tape*

E. Communicative Activities

The Projects, instructions, forms, and readings*

Materials in this book are marked with an asterisk

Contents

Lesson 1: Freddy Gallagher, bank teller

Introductory Reading

It is easy to understand why a young man or woman, a recent graduate of high school, could be attracted to a job in a bank: pleasant working conditions in an attractive building, no special experience necessary, on-the-job training, health and dental insurance (after thirty days of employment in most banks), retirement benefits, paid holidays and vacations, opportunities for advancement (a person might even become president of the bank fifteen or twenty years down the line), and then, there's the feeling of power that comes from being surrounded by all that money.

But, the next time you are waiting in line to withdraw or deposit money, take a close look at what is required of that teller: she or he needs to be extraordinarily accurate (notice how the fingers fly over the computer keys and also all the counting of bills that is necessary), and she or he needs to have much better than average ability to work with numbers and the ability to work quickly and accurately, especially during those rush times when suddenly the bank is filled with customers who are not-so-patiently waiting their turn.

In addition, this constant working with money, often large sums of it, would seem to require extra amounts of concentration. And certainly, flexibility of mind is important. Why? What about those times, for example, when the computer system that everyone depends on for all aspects of the work suddenly is "down!" and it is necessary to remain pleasant and helpful to all the potentially very impatient customers.

In the town of Brattleboro, Vermont, where Freddy lives, there are approximately 50 tellers working in seven different banks. Only four of these tellers are men. The job clearly is attracting far more women in this community these days. But there are other reasons why Freddy isn't your usual bank teller in Brattleboro. He's going to tell you about it. ℒ

Work Related Vocabulary

These words or phrases are used in the interview you're about to hear. In groups discuss the vocabulary, sharing knowledge and using a dictionary when needed. Check (✓) off those words you already know. If a word or phrase is new to you and you want to learn it, in the space beside it either write its meaning in English or in your own language or write an English sentence using it.

1.   a bank teller ✓
2.   a time card
3.   a vault
4.   cash and change ✓
5.   a deposit slip ✓
6.   a withdrawal slip ✓
7.   credit and debit slips ✓
8.   paper clips ✓
9.   a rubber stamp ✓
10. an ink pad ✓
11. to sign on (to a computer)
12. a station
13. a teller number ✓
14. a secret code number ✓
15. to access (me to the computer)
16. to punch in
17. an account number ✓
18. transactions ✓
19. the computer is down ✓
20. passbooks ✓
21. loans ✓
22. money orders ✓
23. interest rates ✓

Additional vocabulary

1.   repetitive
2.   an ESL book
3.   automatic
4.   to revolutionize

 # The Interview

Tape: Part One—The first listening 1

Listen to the interview trying to get a general understanding, the gist, of what the discussion is about and then answer the following questions:

Questions

1. What did you learn about Freddy and his work in this first listening?

2. What are the most interesting things you learned about Freddy and his work?

3. Did anything you learned from the interview surprise you?

 # Vocabulary in Context

Tape: Part Two—listening exercise 2

Listen to the recording and write down the word or phrase you hear. You will hear the word or phrase twice. Then, listen to two sentences in which that word or phrase is used. (The second sentence is taken from the conversation you have heard.) Next, write down what you think that word or phrase means. Make an intelligent guess, using context clues.

1. Listen and write: _____
   Meaning:

2. Listen and write: _____
   Meaning:

3. Listen and write: _____
   Meaning:

4. Listen and write: _____
   Meaning:

5. Listen and write: _____
   Meaning:

6. Listen and write: _____
   Meaning:

Now that you have done the vocabulary in context, listen to the interview again.

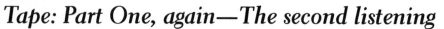 # The Interview

 1

Tape: Part One, again—The second listening

Reconstruction

All of the following words or phrases appear, chronologically, in the interview. Working with a partner, tell something interesting or significant about the word or phrase, as it relates to the interview. For example: "typical day." Possible reconstruction: "Freddy tells what he does on a typical day in the bank."

1. a man in a woman's world
2. stick out like a sore thumb
3. no big deal
4. a dreamer
5. pulling my leg
6. special help
7. loans
8. automatic
9. freer
10. vacations; weekends
11. dreams
12. a poet

4

 # The Dialogue

Tape: Part Three—Freddy and Mr. Holtz

Listen to this conversation. Answer the following questions:

Questions

1. What opportunity is offered to Freddy?

2. What does Freddy decide?   Why?

3. Is Freddy's decision good for the bank?

The Interactive Listening

 4

Tape: Part Four—Are you good at numbers?

There are three parts to this interactive listening exercise. Listen to the tape. In the first part, you will hear ten figures (amounts of money). Compare what you hear with the figures listed below. If the amount below is correct, put a check next to it. If not, write the correct figure.

1. $24.11 _____
2. $989.02 _____
3. $1024.24 _____
4. $1545.20 _____
5. $1042.25 _____
6. $10,876.24 _____
7. $.56 _____
8. $2,000,065.00 _____
9. $123,456.78 _____
10. $5,000,000.00 _____

In the second part of this exercise, five numbers will be read to you, five amounts of money. Take them in dictation.

1. _____
2. _____
3. _____
4. _____
5. _____

In the third part, you must help our interviewer find the error in his checkbook and correct his balance. Listen to his conversation with Freddy.

			(−)	√	(−)	(+)	BALANCE	
CHECK NO.	DATE	CHECKS ISSUED TO OR DESCRIPTION OF DEPOSIT	AMOUNT OF CHECK	T	CHECK FEE (IF ANY)	AMOUNT OF DEPOSIT	476	00
121	3/14	paycheck				623	623	
							1099	
ABT	3/14		50				50	
							1059	
122	3/16	New England Telephone	47				47	00
							1106	10
Dep	3/18	birthday check				100	100	00
							1206	00
123	3/18	bookstore	25	11			25	11
							1180	89
124	3/18	Cash	100				100	00
							1080	89
125	3/20	supermarket	26	28			26	28
							1054	61
	3/21	paycheck				623	623	00
							1677	61
ABT	3/21		50	00			50	
							1627	61
	3/22	refund				10	10	00
							1727	61

PLEASE BE SURE TO **DEDUCT** ANY PER CHECK CHARGES OR SERVICE CHARGES THAT MAY APPLY TO YOUR ACCOUNT

REMEMBER TO RECORD AUTOMATIC PAYMENTS / DEPOSITS ON DATE AUTHORIZED.

			(−)	√	(−)	(+)	BALANCE	
CHECK NO.	DATE	CHECKS ISSUED TO OR DESCRIPTION OF DEPOSIT	AMOUNT OF CHECK	T	CHECK FEE (IF ANY)	AMOUNT OF DEPOSIT		

PLEASE BE SURE TO **DEDUCT** ANY PER CHECK CHARGES OR SERVICE CHARGES THAT MAY APPLY TO YOUR ACCOUNT

REMEMBER TO RECORD AUTOMATIC PAYMENTS / DEPOSITS ON DATE AUTHORIZED.

The Projects

A *choice of communicative activities*

Choose one of the following projects. You may work alone or with one or two classmates.

Project One

Go into two banks. In each find out how to open a checking account. Find out what the monthly costs are of having a checking account in each bank. Under what circumstances will they pay interest? Bring back forms so that you can tell your classmates what information they must provide to the bank before they can open an account. Tell them which bank you prefer and why.

Project Two

Interview five people about what differences they find between banking in their country and in the country where they are now living. Organize your information and report it to the class.

Project Three

Go into two banks and find out how to get a loan to buy a car. Find out what information you must give them when applying for a loan, and what assets you must have before they will give you a loan. Find out about interest rates, additional charges, time given to pay off the loan, and any other questions you may have. Bring back forms for your classmates to see. Tell them which bank you would prefer to get the loan from and why.

Project Four

If you know anyone who works in a bank, interview him or her. Prepare interesting questions before you do your interview. Afterwards, organize what you learned into a report and present it to the class. Here is a sample question: Why did you choose to work in a bank?

Project Five

Poll ten people. Ask them if they agree or disagree with the ten statements you present to them. Organize the data and present it to the class. Here are six sample statements. You may use these or make up ten of your own.

1. Banks never make mistakes.
2. I often use an automated banking machine when I need cash.
3. I usually deposit money into an automated banking machine.
4. Automated banking machines never make mistakes.
5. Banking is a noble business and one can compare bank presidents to heads of hospitals.
6. Bankers and banks are completely honest institutions.

Project Six

Interview two elderly people. Ask them if banking has changed in their lifetimes and, if so, how. Compare their answers and organize what you learn into a report. You might invite one or both people to visit your class to help with your report. Work out with them what questions you will ask them in front of the class.

Project Seven

Read the following article about jobs in a bank. It is the text of a brochure written for high school students who may be thinking about a career in banking. Because this is the transcription of a tape, it is oral rather than written language. As a result, it is sometimes ungrammatical and there are many sentence fragments.

After you have read the brochure, tell the class about it, comparing it to what Freddy Gallagher says in the interview. Prepare a vocabulary lesson for the class. List separately words and phrases related to banking like "deposit slips" and other interesting vocabulary like "on the job training" and "myth".

A Career in Banking Is It for YOU?

INTRODUCTION: WHAT IT'S ACTUALLY LIKE

I Am a Teller

I am employed by a medium sized bank. I have a high school education.

I had good school marks at high school, but could not afford to go to college. My school counselor told me about on the job training for tellers at this bank. And that the bank was looking for new applicants. I applied for a job and was accepted. It was the best thing that could have happened to me at that time.

My only direct contact with banks before being employed here, was to make small deposits in my savings account. My new job was a fast learning experience for me.

For example, I'd always thought banks opened at ten and closed at three, the business hours posted outside the bank where I deposited. That myth was ended immediately. I learned I had to be on the job an hour early and leave when my after hours duties were completed. These usually take at least an hour.

Other things I learned too, during my training for this work. They included being told that I must dress conservatively; be well groomed. That the bank's employees were its representatives. As such, my appearance at the teller's counter should enhance the bank's image.

Training included instruction in such pre-opening teller duties as counting cash in my drawer, making certain rubber stamps, deposit slips and other things I'd need were in good order.

All during training it was stressed that the bank

9

expected me to be pleasant with customers while rendering the best services of which I was capable. That any questions I couldn't answer I should either ask someone, another employee, or direct the customer to another department where the information might be available.

Primarily I take care of customer deposits and withdrawals. I must check to verify deposit totals, after seeing to it that all checks involved are accurately made out and endorsed, and any cash, counted. Once the deposit is verified and receipted, the deposit slip is placed with the checks to be sent to the proof department. A receipt is also given the depositor.

Whenever withdrawals are made, I must be meticulous about counting out the cash to the customer. Accuracy is my responsibility.

Use of computers is a part of my job. Whenever I need to verify if a customer's account will cover a check, verify a signature, or need other information, I turn to the computer.

I enjoy meeting customers and try to give them services that will justify my job. By closing time I am usually tired from hours on my feet and trying not to show it. I still have my after closing duties to perform.

These include counting the cash and checking it against the balance sheet before asking my supervisor, the head teller, to check it too. Then I sort all the deposit and withdrawal slips and the checks, before sending them on to other departments for recording and clearing.

It takes time and some skills to learn to do this job right. Now I'm taking evening courses at the community college. I'm also signed up to take banking association courses. I don't want to stay being a teller. And I don't have to. Not in the banking industry. You can go as far as your ambition, talents and other qualifications will take you.

POSITIVE ASPECTS

Diversification and numbers of job opportunities in banking are often cited as the most positive aspects of this career. Not only do these aspects appeal to ambitious bank careerists, they also attract professionals outside traditional banking.

Incentives offered in banking careers are many. Incentives that include inducements toward continual career education and advancement.

On the job training can be a most positive aspect. Particularly for careerists who have had no opportunity for education toward banking.

There is job security in banking for the qualified.

There is the security of knowing that banking is expected to continue to grow.

Changes that are always occuring keep many stimulated and interested.

Some are attracted by specifics and types of work. Currently this includes electronics; automatic tellers, computers and other machines, which open up an entire new range of career possibilities.

Rotation in jobs and transfers are sometimes cited as attractive to some. There is the opportunity to change employment, go to another bank, or move location.

Challenges that are a constant in banking attract those who like to be challenged.

Keeping in touch with the financial world and what is going on in the community can be fascinating aspects of this work.

Meeting and dealing with all types of people give career impetus to the field for others.

Providing services for others is a satisfying aspect for those who enjoy helping others.

Team effort is sometimes cited as agreeable.

Meeting and working with professionals in other fields can be stimulating.

Meeting and working with professionals in other fields can be stimulating and enjoyable for some in executive positions.

Banking offers many opportunities for promotion to executive and high administration positions.

Individual endeavor at some levels of employment can be a most agreeable aspect for those who enjoy such aspects as researching credit ratings, customers' ability to repay loans, others.

The one aspect often cited as most attractive is the wide diversification of job opportunities. This provides jobs for prospective careerists of many differing talents, educational backgrounds and also provides opportunities for setting new banking career goals.

NEGATIVE ASPECTS

There is mental stress connected with many jobs in banking. Bankers may cite their responsibility for the assets of others as most demanding.

Physical stress occurs when work includes hours of standing and walking.

Job rotation and department transfers that can be a part of this work, particularly if the bank is large with many branches, are unattractive for some. Especially those who prefer to work in one department or in one location.

Customer complaints that are sometimes difficult to deal with such as checking accounts they can't seem to balance, investments that don't meet expectations, inability to make payments on loans, can become a most disagreeable aspect of this work.

Seminars and other training sessions to keep personnel abreast of current trends and to update expertise generally, seem unattractive to some.

In-bank competition for upper level employment can be a source of friction.

Changes that impact their jobs directly, make some unhappy. Particularly when they mean having to learn new procedures and skills.

Some negative aspects may apply more to certain levels of employment. For example, those in management may have to spend considerable time outside banking hours to make contacts, attend organizational meetings and community events. They may see these as time consuming and physically draining. Some may even seem unnecessary.

Having to perform maximally to give best services possible to customers, and maintain a smile and pleasant attitude, no matter how tired they are, may be cited by tellers as trying.

QUALIFICATIONS

Besides your training and education you will require other skills and qualifications if you expect to succeed in this career field. For example, a sense of responsibility will be needed for almost any job pursued in banking. Especially for those involved in management, administration and other functions concerned directly with the money and financial arrangements of others.

A liking for people and desire to be of service, are among other qualifications basic to banking.

Honesty and integrity are both important qualifications.

Ability to communicate is of vital importance. To inform customers and others concerning the bank's services, and to instruct them in such aspects as the use of teller machines.

Ability to work under stress is necessary in some of this work.

Ability to work cooperatively with others can be another important qualification.

Good health is necessary.

Good judgment and attention to details are other basic qualifications to be considered.

Ability to program and use electronic equipment such as computers and data processors is important.

Tact and diplomacy in handling financial arrangements and dealing directly with people, is of utmost importance.

Some qualifications apply importantly to a particular aspect of banking. Some of these include:

Dedication to community often required of managers and others seeking new business for the bank.

Well groomed and pleasant appearance is a requirement for tellers.

Ability to maintain hours of concentrated effort toward putting together and analyzing data and other information can be a most important qualification for a banking career.

Credit: The Institute for Research, Northfield, Illinois

11

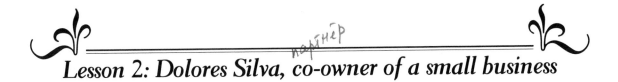

Lesson 2: Dolores Silva, co-owner of a small business

Introductory Reading

W ho is there among us who hasn't dreamed of having his or her own small (maybe, eventually, even big) business, and having wonderful freedom, both from a boss and from the time clock: the freedom to make up our own rules for our work, and our own schedule—arranging our own hours of work? That way work would be both painless and fun. Or, so we imagine.

Well, in reality it isn't quite as simple as that. Yes, it is true that being the boss has its satisfactions and that working hours can be more flexible if you own your own small business. But in those early years of getting your own business off the ground, you shouldn't count on taking a day off, let alone flying off for a month's vacation. It is not unusual for new business owners to work seventy or eighty hours a week, and if there is a day off, that day might need to be devoted to getting caught up on accounting.

But this negative picture doesn't deter the hopefuls. The possibility of wonderful rewards—both financial and psychological—continues to motivate that large number of people who start up small business operations each year in the United States.

In this chapter you will get acquainted with Dolores Silva, who with her co-owner husband, Ben, is part of the group of those who are making a go of a small business enterprise. They have been in business almost three years now. It isn't easy. This interview with Dolores will give you an idea of what that life is really like. ൙

Work Related Vocabulary

These words or phrases are used in the interview you're about to hear. In groups discuss the vocabulary, sharing knowledge and using a dictionary when needed. Check (✓) off those words you already know. If a word or phrase is new to you and you want to learn it, in the space beside it either write its meaning in English or in your own language or write an English sentence using it.

1. a co-owner
2. a business manager
3. a sales person
4. an accountant
5. a janitor
6. arts and crafts objects
7. wholesale
8. to import
9. correspondence
10. to go over the books
11. a Spring sale
12. to make an offer
13. a special offer
14. a bargain
15. profit
16. profit margin
17. retail
18. inventory

Additional vocabulary

1. to overwhelm
2. variety
3. gruff
4. the flu
5. dumb
6. to apologize
7. persuasion
8. to skip lunch
9. to unload
10. a cough

14

 # The Interview

Tape: Part One—The first listening 1

Listen to the interview trying to get a general understanding, the gist, of what the discussion is about and then answer the following questions:

Questions

1. What did you learn about Dolores and her work in this first listening?

2. What are the most interesting things you learned about Dolores and her work?

3. Did anything you learned from the interview surprise you?

 # Vocabulary in Context

Tape: Part Two—listening exercise 2

Listen to the recording and write down the word or phrase you hear. You will hear the word or phrase twice. Then, listen to two sentences in which that word or phrase is used. (The second sentence is taken from the conversation you have heard.) Next, write down what you think that word or phrase means. Make an intelligent guess, using context clues.

1. Listen and write: _____
   Meaning:

2. Listen and write: _____
   Meaning:

3. Listen and write: _____
   Meaning:

4. Listen and write: _____
   Meaning:

5. Listen and write: _____
   Meaning:

6. Listen and write: _____
   Meaning:

Now that you have done the vocabulary in context, listen to the interview again.

The Interview

Tape: Part One, again—The second listening ✹ 1

Reconstruction

All of the following words or phrases appear, chronologically, in the interview. Working with a partner, tell something interesting or significant about the word or phrase, as it relates to the interview. For example: "Mexico." Possible reconstruction: "Mexico is a country in North America from which the Silvas import many arts and crafts things."

1. co-owners
2. especially janitor
3. arts and crafts objects
4. wholesale
5. go over the books
6. took his temperature
7. all hell broke loose
8. Tomas Martin
9. Spring sale
10. turned down his offer
11. a deep, gruff voice
12. grumbling about this and that
13. he sniffed
14. feminine charm
15. birthday or Christmas gifts

 # The Dialogue

 3

Tape: Part Three—Dolores and Heftig

Listen to this conversation. Answer the following questions:

Questions

1. What do you know about the man's attitude towards women from this conversation? How do you know this? Have you ever encountered a situation like this?

2. Words like "Baby," "Honey," and "Sweetheart" are usually very nice terms. Why is Dolores Silva very insulted by his use of them?

3. Summarize the gist of the dialogue.

The Interactive Listening

Tape: Part Four—Taking an order by phone ✳ 4

Several months have passed. Once again Dolores gets a call from Tomas Martin in Mexico. Listen in on her conversation and, as she gives her order to Tomas, fill out his order form below.

Martin & Frank
Export/Import
Regalos Typicos Native Arts & Crafts

ITEM	Quantity	Price/item	Special price	Total
ORDER FORM. SEASON: CHRISTMAS ORDER DATE: PURCHASE ORDER #				
ties (knit)				
ties (printed)				
hats (children)				
hats (adults)				
sweater (child sm.)				
sweater (" medium)				
sweater (" large)				
sweater (men sm.)				
sweater (" medium)				
sweater (" large)				
sweater (women sm.)				
sweater (" medium)				
sweater (" large)				
skirts				
woven handbags				
leather bags				
leather wallets				
coffee mugs (red)				
coffee mugs (blue)				
3 bowls, set (red)				
boxes (animals)				
tops (animals)				
picture frames				
dolls (Mexican)				
tablecloth set				
marimbas				
rattles (gourd)				
rattles (wood)				
belt buckles				
creche figures				
5 tree ornaments				
			TOTAL	

The Projects

A *choice of communicative activities*

Choose one of the following projects. The projects in this lesson involve working together in groups, planning interviews with people, arranging for the interviews, conducting them, and presenting the results to the class. The four steps suggested below can be followed for any of these projects.

Step 1: Sit together in a small group, discuss the project, and design questions for the interview. Be sure everyone understands what information you want, what questions you will ask, and who will ask them. There are many ways to ask questions: Example A. What different kinds of work do you do? Example B. Do you do any of the following during the day—answering the telephone, accounting. A good way to test your interview design is to let one of your group pretend to be the person you are going to interview and to role play the interview with him or her.

Step 2: Decide how to find someone to interview. Perhaps someone in the group knows someone. Perhaps you can ask the owner of a store where you shop. One of you should arrange the interview. You will be surprised how delighted people usually are to be asked about themselves. Tell the person exactly what you're working on and a little bit about the information you need. Arrange for a specific time, and arrive on time.

Step 3: All persons in the group should be at the interview. Listen carefully to what the person who is being interviewed is saying. Have your questions ready, but don't stick rigidly to them. Decide beforehand who will take notes. If you decide to tape the interview, get the person's permission ahead of time.

Step 4: Discuss the interview in your group and organize the material to present to the class.

Project One

Interview someone who has a small business. (restaurant, card shop, shoemaker, pet store, etc.) Find out all the different kinds of work they do in their business and how many hours a day they devote to it. Find out if they have any help. Find out what kind of background they have and how they ended up in this particular business. Ask them about the advantages and disadvantages of owning a small business, etc. etc.

Project Two

Interview someone who is a partner or a co-owner in a small family run business (husband/wife; brother/sister). The focus of your interview is on the advantages and disadvantages of working many hours a day with someone in your family.

Project Three

Interview five people. Find out if any of them are small business owners or the children of small business owners, or if they have ever dreamed of owning their own small businesses. Find out what small businesses they dream about. Design your questions so that you get their opinions, for example, on the advantages and disadvantages of small business ownership.

Lesson 3: Neal Wade, waiter

Introductory Reading

In order to understand and perhaps even "appreciate" the work done by Neal, a waiter, consider the following questions before you listen to the interview with him.
Recollect one of your recent experiences in a restaurant. Why were you eating in a restaurant on this particular occasion? (Business, getting some food in a hurry, having a relaxed meal before or after a cultural event, having an evening out of the house, saving the trouble of preparing a meal . . .) For what reason(s) did you choose the restaurant you went to? What do you remember about the workers in the restaurant? What work do you recall them doing? Describe the waiter and tell as much as you can about him or her. What are your expectations of a waiter? How do you expect that person to relate to you? Do you consider that your waiter did a good job? Why or why not?

Describe the best waiter who ever served you. Also describe the worst waiter who ever served you.

Neal is one of an army of people who work as waiters in the seemingly infinite variety of restaurants in the United States. Yes, you find everything from McDonald's and Pizza Hut and Kentucky Fried Chicken (fast food franchises) to the most deluxe dining areas in expensive hotels. Who are these people who have chosen to be waiters? Well, there are:

■ men and women of every age for whom waiting provides their sole means of income; mothers working part-time, providing a second income; single mothers and single fathers;

■ college students from virtually every economic background putting in a summer in their local communities, or if they are somewhat adventuresome, working in either plain or fancy summer resorts (on Cape Cod in Massachusetts, for example) or at an inn or lodge in a national park (Yellowstone is one of the favorites). Many college students also work weekends or evenings during the school year to earn tuition money;

■ multitudes of high school students, working an after-school shift at pizza parlors, Burger King, or any of the many fast food emporiums. Technically, they are not waiters but counter people. For many it is their first taste of work. They get the legal minimum wage and do not get the tips which can make waiting a lucrative job.

Neal has been a waiter for many years. He's going to tell you about his work. As you listen, consider whether or not you would like him to wait on you. ✑

Work Related Vocabulary

These words or phrases are used in the interview you're about to hear. In groups discuss the vocabulary, sharing knowledge and using a dictionary when needed. Check (✓) off those words you already know. If a word or phrase is new to you and you want to learn it, in the space beside it either write its meaning in English or in your own language or write an English sentence using it.

1. a bus boy
2. tips
3. a fridge
4. a flexible schedule
5. a shift
6. time off
7. prep work
8. to set (up) the table
9. specials
10. bread warmers
11. rare meat
12. well-done meat
13. an order of fries
14. a stressful job
15. decaf

Additional vocabulary

1. a run
2. iffy (business)
3. to cater to

The Interview

 1

Tape: Part One—The first listening

Listen to the interview trying to get a general understanding, the gist, of what the discussion is about and then answer the following questions:

Questions

1. What did you learn about Neal and his work in this first listening?

2. What are the most interesting things you learned about Neal?

3. Did anything you heard in the interview surprise you?

Vocabulary in Context

 2

Tape: Part Two—Listening exercise

Listen to the recording and write down the word or phrase you hear. You will hear the word or phrase twice. Then, listen to two sentences in which that word or phrase is used. (The second sentence is taken from the conversation you have heard.) Next, write down what you think that word or phrase means. Make an intelligent guess, using context clues.

1. Listen and write: _____
   Meaning:

2. Listen and write: _____
   Meaning:

3. Listen and write: _____
   Meaning:

4. Listen and write: _____
   Meaning:

5. Listen and write: _____
   Meaning:

6. Listen and write: _____
   Meaning:

Now that you have done the vocabulary in context, listen to the interview again.

✳ The Interview

Tape: Part One, again—The second listening 1

Reconstruction

Working with a partner, comment on each of the following phrases that you heard in the interview. Give the context for the phrase and explain as fully as possible what the person was talking about.

1. teaching English
2. on and off
3. an iffy business
4. the Fifth Season
5. my fridge is empty
6. It's mindless
7. Noises Off
8. the prep work
9. a business lunch
10. burn out
11. a stressful job
12. stay tuned in

The Dialogue

Tape: Part Three—Neal and Louise  3

Listen to this conversation. Answer the following questions:

Questions

1. Describe Louise's problems.

2. How does Neal respond to these problems?

3. Summarize the main point of the dialogue.

The Interactive Listening

 4

Tape: Part Four—Taking Orders

The waitress Louise is waiting on four people who are having lunch at the Fifth Season. You are going to recognize some or all of these people. Listen to their conversation and take down their orders on the checks below. After you have checked out the prices on the menu on the next page, add up the bill for each person. Be sure to add the 5% state sales tax charged on all meals in this state.

Matt

The Fifth Season		
Thank you Louise	Subtotal	
	State meals tax 5%	
	TOTAL	

Andy

The Fifth Season		
Thank you Louise	Subtotal	
	State meals tax 5%	
	TOTAL	

Elise

The Fifth Season		
Thank you Louise	Subtotal	
	State meals tax 5%	
	TOTAL	

Ed

The Fifth Season		
Thank you Louise	Subtotal	
	State meals tax 5%	
	TOTAL	

The Fifth Season
Lunch or Brunch

Today's Menu

Toasted Three Deckers

SLICED ROAST TURKEY CLUB	3.95	BACON CHEESEBURGER SPECIAL CLUB 3.75
RARE ROAST BEEF AND CHEDDAR CLUB	3.95	TUNAFISH SALAD CLUB ...... 3.75 CLASSIC CHICKEN CLUB 3.75
SLICED HAM AND CHEESE CLUB	3.50	

Salad Platters

ALBACORE TUNAFISH SALAD	3.75
ZORBA'S GREEK SALAD WITH FETA CHEESE & OLIVES	2.95
CHEF'S SALAD BOWL—HAM, TURKEY, CHEESE & SLICED EGG	3.75
Chunky Bleu Cheese Dressing	.25 extra

From the Sandwich Board

OPEN REUBEN, ORIGINAL DELI DELIGHT Corned Beef, Swiss Cheese and Sauerkraut on Pumpernickel and served with French Fries	3.75
CHAR-BROILED HAMBURGER (¼ lb.)	1.95
CHAR-BROILED CHEESEBURGER (¼ lb.)	1.95
With Lettuce and Tomato	2.20
BROOKLYN'S HOT PASTRAMI ON A BULKIE ROLL	2.75
With Swiss Cheese	3.25
GRILLED CHEESE & HAM or BACON	1.85
GRILLED SWISS CHEESE & HAM	2.10
FRIED EGG with HAM	1.85
WESTERN or EASTERN	1.85
BACON, LETTUCE & TOMATO ON TOAST	1.85
FRESH CHICKEN SALAD	2.25
COLD SLICED TURKEY or COLD ROAST BEEF	2.95
TWO FOOT TWO—THE GRINDER, SUB, OR HOGIE OF YOUR DESIRE	4.50

From the Grill

HAM, BACON or SAUSAGE AND EGGS	2.75	FETA CHEESE OMELETTE	3.00
CHEESE OMELETTE	2.75	WESTERN OMELETTE	2.75
SWISS CHEESE OMELETTE	3.00	SPANISH OMELETTE	3.00
		MUSHROOM OMELETTE	3.00
GRILLED JUNIOR SIRLOIN STEAK AND TWO EGGS			4.85

Above Orders served with Toast and Potatoes

GRANNY'S OWN BUTTERMILK PANCAKES WITH BACON or SAUSAGE	2.75
GRANNY'S OWN BUTTERMILK PANCAKES WITH TWO FRIED EGGS	2.75
GRILLED FRENCH TOAST WITH BACON or SAUSAGE	2.75

Side Orders

The Chef's Salad - Small	95
Large	1.50
Our Famous French Fried Potatoes	.75
Creative Cole Slaw	.40
Vegetables du jour	.40
Fresh Baked Potato	.75
Mama's 3-Bean Salad	.60
Incredible Onion Rings	.85

Beverages

Wine, a glass of red or white	2.00
Beer, domestic	1.50
Beer, imported	2.00
Coffee, Tea or Decaf (Sanka)	.55
Iced Tea or Coffee	.55
Milk	.50
Coke, Sprite, Tab, Lemonade	.45

Appetizers

Orange or Apple Juice	.50-.75
Tomato Juice	.50-.75
Grapefruit Juice	.50-.75
Fresh Fruit Cup with Sherbet	1.00
Shrimp Cocktail	Each Shrimp .75
Potato Skins With Cheese Stuffing	2.00
Papa's Spicy Onion Toasts	2.00
Baker's Dozen Pizza Puffs	3.50
Mama's Stock-Pot Special Soup, cup	1.00
bowl	2.00

The Chef's Specialties

BROILED NEW YORK SIRLOIN STEAK, Chef's Salad and Potato	7.50
BROILED FRESH PORK CHOPS, Apple Sauce, Chef's Salad and Potato	4.95
GRILLED JUNIOR SIRLOIN STEAK, Chef's Salad and Potato	4.95
BROILED HALF OF SPRING CHICKEN, Chef's Salad and Potato	4.95
VEAL CUTLET PARMESAN AND SPAGHETTI	5.50
VEAL CUTLET AND EGGPLANT PARMESAN with Spaghetti	6.00
VEAL CUTLET AND SPAGHETTI	5.00
EGGPLANT PARMESAN and Spaghetti or Chef's Salad	3.75
CHAR-BROILED CHOPPED SIRLOIN OF BEEF with Onions, Chef's Salad and Potato	3.95
ROAST TOP OF THE ROUND, AU JUS with Chef's Salad and Potato	4.25

Fresh from the Sea

Served with Cole Slaw or Salad and French Fries

BROILED FILLET OF SOLE	3.95
BROILED BOSTON SCHROD	4.75
BROILED SEA SCALLOPS, Drawn Butter	6.00
FRIED FRESH GULF SHRIMP	5.50
FRIED FRESH CLAMS, Tartar Sauce	5.50
FRIED SEA SCALLOPS, Tartar Sauce	6.00
FRESH AFRICAN LOBSTER TAILS	7.00
MIXED SEAFOOD PLATTER	7.00
SWORDFISH (in season)	
SHADROE (in season)	
BUSTER SOFT SHELL CRABS (in season)	

Desserts

OH-MY-WHAT-A-PUDDING WITH CREAM	.85
FRUIT JELLO WITH CREAM	.50
GRANNY'S GREAT PIES A LA MODE	Extra .60
DISH OF BEN & JERRY'S ICE CREAM or SHERBET	.90
AMERICANA APPLE PIE	1.00
DEATH BY CHOCOLATE	1.50
FLAN	1.00
CHOCOLATE DREAM CREAM PIE	1.00
OUR OWN TOP BANANA CREAM PIE	1.00

All Granny's Pies and Pastries are baked on the Premises Daily

(*Please note: This menu is not actually from the Fifth Season Restaurant)

The Projects

A *choice of communicative activities*

Choose one of the following projects. You may work alone or with one or two classmates.

Project One

Be a close observer. Have you ever watched a waiter or waitress at work? Have you ever considered what the steps are in serving just one table? You are about to do some careful observation. Either alone or with a classmate go to a restaurant. Bring pencil and paper with you. Choose a waiter or waitress to observe and make notes on what this waiter or waitress does from the time you begin observing him or her until the time you leave. Organize your notes to present to the class.

Project Two

Interview a waiter or a waitress. Prepare a list of relevant questions that you might ask. You will probably want to know about the advantages and drawbacks of the job, what other work this person has done, as well as many other work related questions. Organize your notes and present the information from the interview to the class.

Project Three

Poll students from different countries about waiters and waitresses in their countries or about waiters and waitresses in the country you're in. Present the results of polling ten people to the class. Invent about ten questions. Here are some sample true or false questions, but feel free to make up any kind of questions you want.

1. In the United States, working as a waiter or waitress is not considered a respectable job even if it is at a very expensive restaurant and even if the person makes more money than a teacher does. (True or false?)

2. Your parents would be pleased if you worked as a waiter or a waitress part-time in order to help pay for your education. (True or false?)

3. Waiter and waitresses usually do not have very good educations. (True or false?)

Project Four

Interview five people about what it is that pleases them about a waiter and waitress when they go to a restaurant for a leisurely meal and what it is that annoys them. Although you may not need them, prepare interesting leading questions to help the people being interviewed. Organize the information noting similarities in responses and report back to the class.

Project Five

Read the following article. Prepare a vocabulary lesson from the reading to teach the class. Also compare some of this to what Neal has said in his interview. Present the material and the vocabulary lesson to the class. Discuss whether the same things are rude and appropriate in your native country.

In the introduction to this chapter, you were asked to recall a recent experience in a restaurant. You were asked to think about what waiters sometimes do that annoys you. You have heard Neal talk about his customers and the kinds of things they do that annoy him. Now here is another perspective on this subject: What most annoys managers and hostesses about the people who come to be served?

=====

What Annoys a Restaurateur the Most

Jonathan at the Fifth Season:

We take great pride in our work here. We want to get the order right. We want to satisfy the customer. I get especially annoyed when customers complain to me — as they are paying the bill at the end of the evening — that the food was not as they wanted it.

That is not the time to complain. The time to say something is when the meal comes or when they discover that something is not as they wanted it. Shortly after our waiters serve the meals they ALWAYS go back to ask if everything is O.K. Now THAT is the time for the complaints. If the meat needs to be cooked longer, if the fish is too dry, if the salad needs more tomatoes or onions, tell us then. Too many people say nothing at that time and wait to do the complaining at the end, when it is too late.

Jonathan adds:

Another thing that annoys me very much. This is NOT a fast food restaurant. I repeat, this is NOT a fast food restaurant. When people come in here they should realize that it takes us time to prepare the food especially for them and we want to get it right and it takes time. When someone orders baked schrod, the waiter explains that it will take about 15 minutes to prepare it. But even then, after that explanation, often customers will complain that they had to wait 15 minutes for the baked schrod. If they can't wait that long, they should order something else that doesn't take that long. As you can see, my voice rises even as I think about this. It is very annoying.

Adele Tetraulet, the Hostess at Walker's Restaurant:

I get very annoyed when customers don't wait to be seated. You know, we have a big sign right by the front door that says, "The hostess will seat you. Please wait." We have our good reasons for asking this. Why can't customers respect that request? Yes, sure, most customers do, but there are others who insist on finding their own tables.

And it is very annoying for the chef and for the waiters and the waitresses — all of us — when customers want to change the menu, want to take something off or put something on one of the meals. On the other hand, the good customers are the enthusiastic ones who are happy to be here and respond to our suggestions and recommendations. These customers often send compliments to the chef.

Others who annoy restaurateurs:

People who phone in reservations and then never come. These people are called "no shows."

People who make a reservation for 7 o'clock and arrive at 8:30, with no explanation or apology. And that table has been empty for most of that time (and of course no income for anyone) and then these late-comers expect to be seated at a table immediately.

People who light up a cigarette in the non-smoking section of the restaurant.

People who don't ask for "separate checks" until the end of the meal, when it is time to pay.

29

Project Six

Read Eddi's and Mary's stories. Tell the class about them, emphasizing the advantages and drawbacks of their jobs. From the stories prepare a vocabulary lesson for the class.

WAITRESS
(Oral Histories)

From **Waitress:** *America's Unsung Heroines, by Leon Elder and Lin Rolens, copyright © 1985 by* **Capra Press,** *Santa Barbara.*

EDDI FREDERICK *(a posh seaside hotel)*: I enjoy the closeness amongst the waitresses. I think it comes from suffering the same indignations and receiving the same pleasures.

As for the customers, I don't like them as well in the morning as I do in the afternoon. People are very peculiar in the morning and they forget that I just woke up too. They want their coffee, lots of coffee, and they are crabby until they get it. People have the weirdest breakfast habits; they invent weird combinations—powdered sugar and berries, or melon and honey. Everything is such a big decision—*one* egg, *one* piece of toast, *one* piece of bacon. And they have these amazing and very serious rituals about eating their eggs—everything from using catsup on scrambled eggs to dipping their toast in fried-egg yolks. To me an egg is an egg, but because this is a fancy place, they come in all dressed up expecting something exciting. Sometimes they even want breakfast served in courses.

For uniforms, we wear the modified tuxedo. Polyester, rain or shine, and when the weather is hot, it's a little torture chamber. Before opening every day, we all line up and the maitre d' looks us over, checks our aprons, and makes us turn them over if they have a spot on them.

I enjoy the whole experience of serving food I am proud of in beautiful surroundings. Also, it's a good experience to serve; I think everybody should have to serve sometime in their life.

Something that I have learned is not to judge people by the tip they give you. I no longer think, "What crumbs—they only left me ten percent." I've learned to accept what comes.

The best tippers are usually men between thirty and fifty who wear designer clothes and dine with other men. Women have a hundred reasons for not tipping well: either you are too pretty or threatening, or they do this at home for free, or they are saving their money to buy something after finishing lunch with their friends.

I want to say one more thing. I mostly feel elegant about what I am doing, working in a beautiful restaurant; it is not something to be ashamed of.

You have a funny kind of power working in a fancy place. Sometimes, the customers think you must be as classy as the restaurant and they want to impress you with their good manners. After all, what else are manners for?

I can tell when people know how to order and when they don't. I know when people order

30

spinach salad because they love spinach salad and I know when they're cheap or afraid to try something new. Sometimes I say, "We usually serve that as an appetizer; it is very small." Also, I won't make much if they order small things, so I try to sell them and applaud them for eating a lot or trying new things, like the manta ray. When I first started, I would get so excited when people ate the best things I would say, "Oh, good."

I haven't served any Conga fish, but then I don't know much about it. I don't think anyone outside of the Cousteau Society knows much about the Conga fish.

Nouvelle portions are small but beautiful to look at, pleasing to taste. One man said, "Nouvelle, hell. This isn't enough to fill up a midget." I said that I guessed the portions were kind of controversial, and he said, "Controversial, huh? You don't get enough to eat, you don't come back. Simple as that." I told my boss and he said, "If they want to eat a lot, they should go to a smorgasbord."

MARY SONG (*a country cafe*): I've had other jobs like office work, but that was a drag. I always come back to this because I like the public and the goings-on. I just like taking care of people; I have a husband and four kids still at home and I wait on them too.

I've been here since 1972, over twelve years. We get mostly old-timers here. In fact, they used to call this place the boardroom because all the farmers and politicians gathered here and talked over the business of the country. A lot of our customers are regulars. If they don't want their regular breakfast, they had better tell me when they come in the door because I'll have their order hanging by the time they sit down.

I never tell anybody off. I come from the old school. One guy did proposition me once. I asked him why he thought he had the right to do that—he wouldn't proposition a nurse or supermarket checker. You have to be friendly to be a waitress and people will sometimes mistake that friendliness, but that doesn't happen too often.

My legs and feet hold up well. The other day my feet hurt, but then I realized I'd written ninety-eight checks that day. We do a lot of side work here too; it takes an hour of our day. On Tuesdays we rotate the catsups and mustards and Fantastik the tables. Wednesdays we wash the windows, clean under the coffee machines, and do all the booths. Thursdays we wash all the salt and pepper shakers, and Fridays we wash the sugar holders. On Saturdays we just try to keep up with the customers.

Lesson 4: Bertha Haynes, elementary school teacher

Introductory Reading

How many of your elementary school teachers can you name? Try it. Which of those teachers was your favorite. Why? Try to describe an incident in that grade that stands out in your memory. Which of those teachers was your least favorite? Why? Can you describe a particularly unpleasant scene from that grade?

From what you can remember about that favorite teacher and her or his teaching, can you think of reasons why she or he would have liked being a teacher? What, do you suppose, were the pleasures and the difficulties for that teacher in particular and elementary school teachers in general?

In this chapter you will become acquainted with Bertha Haynes who has been a teacher for many years. Like most of the other elementary school teachers in this country, her education included a bachelor's degree; she majored in environmental science at Wooster College in Wooster, Ohio. She then went on to study for a master's degree and the necessary teaching certificate, which she received from Keene State College in Keene, New Hampshire. There she studied teaching methods, educational philosophy, and curriculum development, and she did practice teaching under the supervision of an experienced teacher. You will find that her ideas about teaching have changed over the years.

As you listen to the interview with Bertha Haynes, consider whether or not you would want to be her student if you were ten years old again. How would the educational experience in her class be different from the education you received in the fifth grade of your school? ♫

Work Related Vocabulary

These words or phrases are used in the interview you're about to hear. In groups discuss the vocabulary, sharing knowledge and using a dictionary when needed. Check (✓) off those words you already know. If a word or phrase is new to you and you want to learn it, in the space beside it either write its meaning in English or in your own language or write an English sentence using it.

1. modified
2. an open classroom
3. Cherokee Indians
4. a pair of scissors
5. a work contract
6. an assignment
7. a learning disability
8. dyslexia
9. a recess
10. an extended classroom

Additional vocabulary

1. chaotic
2. to growl
3. tell me about it
4. a loom
5. a pattern
6. cops
7. a beat
8. strict

 # The Interview

Tape: Part One—The first listening 1

Listen to the interview trying to get a general understanding, the gist, of what the discussion is about and then answer the following questions:

Questions

1. What did you learn about Bertha and her work, in general and in detail, this first listening?

2. What are the most interesting things you learned about Bertha and her work?

3. Did anything you learned from the interview surprise you?

 # Vocabulary in Context

Tape: Part Two—Listening exercise 2

Listen to the recording and write down the word or phrase you hear. You will hear the word or phrase twice. Then, listen to two sentences in which that word or phrase is used. (The second sentence is taken from the conversation you have heard.) Next, write down what you think that word or phrase means. Make an intelligent guess, using context clues.

1. Listen and write: _____
   Meaning:

2. Listen and write: _____
   Meaning:

3. Listen and write: _____
   Meaning:

Now that you have done the vocabulary in context, listen to the interview again.

 # The Interview

Tape: Part One, again—The second listening 1

Reconstruction

Working with a partner, comment on each of the following phrases that you heard. Give the context for the phrase and explain as fully as possible what the person was talking about:

1. center of attention
2. beehive of activity
3. purposeful
4. Cherokee Indians
5. pair of scissors
6. complicated
7. loom

8. dyslexia
9. fat face
10. police station
11. movable desks
12. enthusiasm
13. Indian bread

 # The Dialogue

 3

Tape: Part Three—Bertha and Mr. Sears

Listen to this conversation. Answer the following questions:

Questions

1. Why did this father come to visit Mrs. Haynes?

2. What does he learn?

3. What is the major surprise?

 # The Interactive Listening

 4

Tape: Part Four—Ed gets interviewed, and so do you.

In this exercise you will meet Dr. Marilyn Jones. Marilyn is the principal of the James Elementary School where Bertha is the fifth grade teacher. Listen to the conversation between Marilyn and Ed and take notes on her questions in the space below. You will then hear a few extra questions. Take notes on these too. Be prepared to answer all of the questions, sharing information about yourself with your classmates. You should also be prepared to share what you have learned about Ed's school days.

1.

2.

3.

4.

5.

6.

7.

8.

9.

10.

11.

12.

13.

14.

15.

16.

17.

18.

 # The Projects

A choice of communicative activities

Choose one of the following projects. You may work alone or with one or two classmates.

Project One

Interview five people about what characteristics they think a good teacher should have (for example, patience). Add your own. Prepare a list for the class of all of the characteristics mentioned. Ask everyone in the class to choose what they consider to be the five most important characteristics mentioned and then discuss this in small groups.

Project Two

Interview a teacher. Prepare relevant questions that you want to ask before the interview, but also listen carefully to what the teacher is saying—that is, the direction of the conversation—and then develop new questions that are of interest. Organize your notes and summarize the information to present to the class. Here are some sample questions: Did you always want to be a teacher? What are some of the advantages of teaching? What are some of the disadvantages? Can you remember your first class?

Project Three

Go to the school of education in a university to get information. Get a brochure. Find out what the requirements are for acceptance and what some of the courses are that future teachers take. Report this information back to the class.

Project Four

Interview a student from another country about the system of education in that country. Prepare questions ahead of time that you might use. Organize your notes. Report on the interview to the class.

Project Five

Poll ten people. Prepare a list of interesting statements and questions to respond to. Organize the responses and report back to the class. Here are some sample statements: Teachers are born, not made. Teachers should never hit students, no matter what the circumstances are. A good teacher should be strict. Anyone can be a good teacher if he knows his subject well. Teachers should be paid as much as doctors.

Project Six

Find out about "extended classrooms." Teachers often plan lessons so that students can learn both in the classroom and in the greater community. An elementary class learning about the role of the police will not only read about them in the classroom, but will also visit a police station and speak to a policeman. They may have to question adults about their interactions with the police, and they may even get to ride in a police car.

Students who are learning about death rituals in various societies might learn such vocabulary as "cemetery, tombstone, undertaker, casket, etc." in the classroom. They might also read about the ceremonies in other cultures. In the community they could visit a cemetery making notes of dates and inscriptions. They might read the obituary pages and see what important information is included. They might answer questions like, "What religious rites are practiced when people die and what is their significance?" "What is considered to be proper behavior at the cemetery?" "How much does death cost from the moment a person dies until burial?"

Pretend you are a teacher. Choose a theme for your class to study. Plan the vocabulary you would want the class to learn, some questions you would want your class to answer, and some activities outside the classroom for your students to do. Present the project to your classmates.

For example, Mika, one of our students, planned to have her students study laundries. The vocabulary she expected them to learn was, "laundry (store), laundromat, laundryman, washing machine, cotton, wool, polyester, linen, silk, nylon, synthetic detergent, drycleaning, flat iron, iron, starch, dryer, hanger, spot, stain, shrinking." She also decided that her students should learn: "1. the temperature of water which works well, 2. the difference between a synthetic detergent and natural soap in cost and effectiveness, 3. the kind of material which should be drycleaned."

39

Fill My Thirst

Lord, fill my thirst for a love that grows
sweeter with time.
Open my heart to the light in her eyes as
they shine.
Give me to her as a true gift of her
love defined,
And make us a life that will ripen like
fruit on the vine.

Lord, fill my days with the freedom to be
what I feel,
And to say what I may, just as long as
what I say is real.
Give me the strength to be true to my
own ideals,
And the wisdom to wait till I know what
each moment reveals.

Lord, fill my purse with only the coins
that I need.
Teach me to give, and never to suffer from greed.
For as I let it go, it flows like a log jam
that's freed,
Like the farmer who sows has an endless supply of new seed.

Lord fill my life with the peace that I
know why I'm here.
Keep my mind free from distractions of
worry and fear.
Life is so easy to see when I keep my head clear.
Lord, give me one chance and I'll show that I'm
deeply sincere.

by Douglas Clegg

41

Lesson 5: Douglas Clegg, folk singer

Introductory Reading

You have been listening to folk singer, Douglas Clegg, sing one of his songs called "Fill My Thirst." You heard him accompanied by some of his musical friends.

Douglas, who is thirty-one years old, is making his living as a folk singer. He grew up in California but now lives in a small town in New Hampshire where he goes from gig to gig, from town to town and city to city, entertaining audiences with his music.

A lover of music and musical instruments all his life, Douglas decided only four years ago that he would stop having music as his hobby and, instead, would devote full time to this great love. "Do what you love," he finally decided.

Douglas is self-employed. He makes all the arrangments for his musical engagements. He does all his own promotion work: he makes the phone calls; he sends out the demonstration music tapes; he visits places that hire musicians as entertainers —clubs, bars, fancy restaurants, shopping centers. He makes his schedule.

In addition, when he starts out for one of his gigs, he carries out to his car all the equipment — the musical instruments and the sound equipment including the speakers and microphone and mixers. Then he carries it all from his car to the place where he will perform. And of course when the performance and the entertaining is over, he does all that carrying again, in reverse.

Now you will hear an interview with Douglas in which he tells about his musical history. Later, in a continuation of the interview, he will tell you about how he writes his songs and especially one song, "California," which has some interesting autobiographical information about him, his family, and some very personal feelings about that place — California — where he was born and grew up. He will then sing that song.

Finally, in a conclusion to the chapter, Douglas — with the interviewer — talks about his work and what his work means to him. ♪

Work Related Vocabulary

These words or phrases are used in the interview you're about to hear. In groups discuss the vocabulary, sharing knowledge and using a dictionary when needed. Check (✓) off those words you already know. If a word or phrase is new to you and you want to learn it, in the space beside it either write its meaning in English or in your own language or write an English sentence using it.

1. a gig
2. various musical instruments:
a. a piano
b. a violin
c. a clarinet
d. a guitar
e. a trumpet
f. a trombone
g. a french horn
h. a mandolin
i. a banjo
j. a flute

Additional vocabulary

1. a hobby
2. a trend
3. a garage sale
4. après ski
5. a pawn shop
6. a passion
7. to snowball ✓
8. to [cook] for a living
9. to last

 # The Interview

Tape: Part One—The first listening 1

Listen to the interview trying to get a general understanding, the gist, of what the discussion is about and then answer the following questions:

Questions

1. What did you learn about Douglas and his musical background and his work?

2. What are the most interesting things you learned about Douglas, his background and work?

3. Did anything you learned from the interview surprise you?

 # Vocabulary in Context

Tape: Part Two—Listening exercise 2

Listen to the recording and write down the word or phrase you hear. You will hear the word or phrase twice. Then, listen to two sentences in which that word or phrase is used. (The second sentence is taken from the conversation you have heard.) Next, write down what you think that word or phrase means. Make an intelligent guess, using context clues.

1. Listen and write: _____
   Meaning:

2. Listen and write: _____
   Meaning:

3. Listen and write: _____
   Meaning:

4. Listen and write: _____
   Meaning:

5. Listen and write: _____
   Meaning:

6. Listen and write: _____
   Meaning:

Now that you have done the vocabulary in context, listen to the interview again.

The Interview

Tape: Part One, again—The second listening

Reconstruction

Working with a partner, comment on each of the following phrases that you heard in the interview. Give the context for the phrase and explain as fully as possible what the person was talking about.

1. a Dutch baby
2. waiting actors
3. "Shine on Harvest Moon"
4. just brothers
5. I'd pick up his guitar . . .
6. in the band
7. snowball
8. French and Chinese
9. a Mexican restaurant
10. Aspen, Colorado
11. après ski
12. I decided I'd go for it.

The Interview continues

 3

Tape: Part Three—Conversation and a song

Listen while Douglas and Ed discuss Douglas' song "California" and then listen to the song. Try to understand the lyrics and then answer the following questions.

Questions

1. What do you learn about Douglas?

2. What do you learn about the background of the song "California?"

3. Can you explain the last line of the song?

45

 # The Interview concludes

Tape: Part Four—The end of the interview 4

Listen to the last part of the interview and then answer the following questions

Questions

1. What are the pleasures and the difficulties of Douglas' work?

2. Can you find a point of similarity in the work of Douglas and the work of Neal?

46

The Interactive Listening

 5

Tape: Part Five—The final song

You are about to hear Douglas sing another of his songs. First listen to the song and try to understand the meaning. This time the words to the song are given in your book, but some of the words have been left out. Listen to the song again and fill in the missing words. Then, answer the questions which follow the song.

You Get What's Coming

With my _____ on the ground and my _____ held high
I walked into town _____ to see if I
Could get me a job working on the line.
I told them I'd even work _____
But the man said, "Boy, we don't need your kind."
He wouldn't even raise his eyes to mine.
He said to me, "Look, don't _____ my time."
So I turned and I left him far _____ .

I hired on as a railroad hand
And travelled all across the land.
In time I came to _____
That winning ain't what makes the _____ .
I took up with an old Chinaman.
We headed south to the Rio Grande.
We got us a pick and a couple of pans,
And we looked for gold in the river _____ .

Rising with the sun.
Work till day is done.
Don't _____ much like fun;
Got to turn and run.

The days were long and we worked like _____
And dreamed of the _____ of _____ made.
Each week we'd go into town to _____
And wait with hope as the dust was weighed.
Barely earned enough to keep us paid.
Not a peso to spend I mean to say.
We never got _____ and we never hit pay,
But we kept it up from day to day.

47

Rising with the sun,
Work till day is done.
Don't _____ much like fun;
Got to turn and run.

Then one day as the sun sank _____,
I dipped in a _____ to _____ my brow.
My head was _____ by a golden glow
That held my gaze like a girlie show.
I let out a whoop and I yelled, "_____"
That echoed all through Mexico.
The stone ran _____ in the sand _____
And me and Chang were now in the dough.

Lazing in the sun
_____ all day long.
Don't it _____ like fun.
No need to run.

In time I rode back through the plains
In a _____ coach on a _____ train.
I came to the town where the man remained
Who wouldn't even give me the _____ __ _____.
I tipped my hat as I _____ champagne.
Then I saw the pain upon his _____.
He was stuck in a life that was so mundane.
He thought for sure he'd go insane.

Rising with the sun,
Work till day is done.
He never has no fun.
Got to turn and run.

1. Why do you think the man said, "Boy, we don't need your kind."

2. What does he mean by "In time I came to understand
   That winning ain't what makes the man."

3. What is the main character's attitude when he returns and meets the man again?

4. What is the meaning of "He was stuck in a life that was so mundane."

The Projects

A *choice of communicative activities*

Choose one of the following projects. You may work alone or with one or two classmates.

Project One

Interview five people about their musical backgrounds. Make up a list of questions before hand and then ask them if they seem to be appropriate or make up other questions during the interviews. When you have finished the interviews, summarize your material, comparing and contrasting what the five people told you. Report this back to the class. Here are some questions that you may want to begin with: 1. Do you play a musical instrument? (What is it? What kind of music do you play?) 2. Did you ever play a musical instrument? (What was it? What kind of music did you play? Why don't you play it anymore?) 3. When you were a child did you ever have music lessons? (For how many years? Why did you stop?)

Project Two

Poll ten or more people. Create questions that show attitudes towards the importance of music and the role it should play in education and people's lives. Report back to the class on the results and the conclusions you have drawn from them. You should have about ten questions in your poll. Here are some samples: 1. Is it more important for the schools to teach mathematics or music? 2. Should musicians receive funding from the state in the same way that Olympic athletes do?

Project Three

Share a song. At one point on the tape the interviewer and Douglas Clegg begin to sing "Shine on Harvest Moon." This is an old American ballad that most Americans know, regardless of their age, and can sing together at parties or around a campfire. Can you think of a song from your country that most people would know? Write down the words to the song for your classmates. Translate it into English for them. Now teach them the song. (Sing or use a tape.)

Project Four

Teach a folk song. If you know a folk song in English, write down the words for your classmates and teach it to them. If you don't know one, ask someone you know to teach you one, and then you teach it to your classmates.

Project Five

Poll ten people about their tastes and preferences in music. Summarize your responses and report the results to the class. You should have about eight questions in your poll. Here are some sample questions: What kind of music do you prefer? Who is your favorite singer? What is your favorite song?

Lesson 6: Helen Chandler, volunteer

Introductory Reading

Helen Chandler, whom you will meet in this chapter, is typical of millions of people living in the United States who volunteer their time and services. Many of these volunteers already have full-time jobs, but they find time in the evenings or on weekends or during their vacations to help some person or group in need. Many other volunteers are retired senior citizens. All of these millions of people give their volunteer work freely; they do not get paid.

They work in an unbelievable variety of situations, providing a great variety of services to a great variety of people. Who is the typical volunteer? Here are some examples:

It is sixty-two year-old Ronda Masen, a volunteer for the Brattleboro, Vermont, hospital, who drives a cancer patient 120 miles round trip for chemotherapy every Friday afternoon; it is Ruth Brinker, sixty-six, who brings nutritious dinners to AIDS patients slowly dying in their homes. . . .

It is Matt Hills, twenty-nine, who volunteers three hours every Saturday morning in a Drop-in-Center where he talks with homeless men who need help in finding a place to live; it is forty-five year-old John Gossage in an Adult Education project teaching Robert, a thirty-eight year-old truck driver, how to read for two hours every Tuesday night; it is retired accountant Lillian Little assisting retired people to fill out the complicated income tax forms. . . .

It is housewife Laura Evans, forty-two, a volunteer with the Parents as Teachers program, assisting the second grade teacher two mornings a week; it is Habitat For Humanity (see page 106) volunteer Linda Blake, eighty-two, helping neighbors build their house; it is Helen Chandler, whom you are about to meet.

Why do they do it? Again, the word is "variety." There is a variety of reasons. There are those who have a religious motivation, believing that their religious faith requires or inspires service to others. Many, who are retired from their regular professional lives, just like to "keep busy." But for almost all of them, there is pleasure in knowing that what they are doing "makes a difference" in the lives of others.

In many ways, Helen Chandler is typical of these volunteers. But like the others, she is unique, too, in ways that may surprise you. ✍

Work Related Vocabulary

These words or phrases are used in the interview you're about to hear. In groups discuss the vocabulary, sharing knowledge and using a dictionary when needed. Check (✓) off those words you already know. If a word or phrase is new to you and you want to learn it, in the space beside it either write its meaning in English or in your own language or write an English sentence using it.

1. a volunteer
2. publicity
3. funding
4. advertising
5. a directory
6. federal agencies
7. a fire hazard
8. an apartment superintendent
9. garbage and trash
10. rent control
11. social welfare
12. a welfare check
13. an addiction
14. an abortion
15. child abuse
16. consumer problems

Additional vocabulary

1. widow
2. luxury
3. a saga
4. defective
5. reputable
6. a flat tire

The Interview

 1

Tape: Part One—The first listening

Listen to the interview trying to get a general understanding, the gist, of what the discussion is about and then answer the following questions:

Questions

1. What did you learn about Helen and her volunteer work in this first listening?

2. What are the most interesting things you learned about Helen and her work?

3. Did anything you learned from the interview surprise you?

Vocabulary in Context

 2

Tape: Part Two—Listening exercise

Listen to the recording and write down the word or phrase you hear. You will hear the word or phrase twice. Then, listen to two sentences in which that word or phrase is used. (The second sentence is taken from the conversation you have heard.) Next, write down what you think that word or phrase means. Make an intelligent guess, using context clues.

1. Listen and write: _____
   Meaning:

2. Listen and write: _____
   Meaning:

3. Listen and write: _____
   Meaning:

4. Listen and write: _____
   Meaning:

5. Listen and write: _____
   Meaning:

6. Listen and write: _____
   Meaning:

Now that you have done the vocabulary in context, listen to the interview again.

The Interview

Reconstruction

Working with a partner, comment on each of the following phrases that you heard in the interview. Give the context for the phrase and explain as fully as possible what the person was talking about.

1. I'm a volunteer.
2. housewife
3. valuable and important
4. Call for Action
5. WBZ
6. huge directory
7. variety of crazy situations
8. elevator
9. a fire hazard
10. the fire department
11. clout
12. social welfare questions
13. refrigerator
14. two flat tires

 # The Dialogue

 3

Helen's phone call to Boston Home Appliances.

You've been asked to write and, perhaps, record your own dialogue.

Topics for discussion or writing

1. Why does Helen volunteer?

2. What would Helen say if you asked her to call businesses in Boston to ask them each to "adopt" an elementary school in a poor country in Latin America, Africa, or Asia? If she said yes, what would she ask the companies to do?

3. What do you think Helen would do if a caller said, "My life is ruined. I'm going to kill myself?"

The Interactive Listening

Tape: Part Four—Finding Jobs for Willing Volunteers 4

Volunteers are needed. Read the descriptions below. Then listen to the seven people on the tape.
Match each person to one of the volunteer jobs below. You are number 8. Choose a job for yourself.
Be prepared to tell your classmates why you matched the each volunteer to his or her job.

DO YOU REALLY CARE?

VOLUNTEERS NEEDED NOW

1. **The American Cancer Society** needs volunteers to staff the *Discovery Shop*, a boutique run by its Brookline/Longwood unit. Donations of clothing and toys are also needed. Call Linda Smith at 278-9125.

2. **The Smithfield V.A. Hospital** needs volunteers to visit veterans who no longer have family or friends living in the area. A two hour a week commitment to the hospital will make a tremendous difference to a lonely veteran. Call Mr. Piers at 564-3221.

3. **The Organization** (Transporting the Handicapped and Elderly) needs both drivers with cars and without cars to drive the handicapped and the elderly to hospitals, clinics and various other medical appointments. Call John at 346-9876.

4. **The Museum of Fine Arts** needs volunteers to guide groups through the various collections in the museum. Become knowledgable about a museum room through several inspiring classes with our experts and share your knowledge and appreciation with our many visitors. Call for an appointment. 631-8976.

5. *School Volunteers Needed.* **The kindergarden, Huntington Public Schools** needs first and second grade volunteers who are willing to assist teachers one morning a week throughout the school year. Call Marilyn Paul, School Volunteer Office, at 981-3344.

6. **Say No to Drugs** needs volunteers to man its crisis intervention hotline from 6:00 to 12:00 P.M. one night a week. Call Gil at 675-3456.

7. **The Arboretum** needs people who enjoy walking and the outdoors to take part in a project to identify early signs of disease in various types of trees. Volunteers will be trained, given an area to investigate, and may do this whenever they have time between now and June 15. Call 892-3435.

8. **Literacy Inc.** needs volunteers. Make the biggest difference in someone's life. We will teach you to teach someone to read so that they can help themselves. Call 234-6789.

9. **Woman's Soup Kitchen** needs volunteers daily to help prepare and serve meals to homeless mothers and childrens. Call Rosie at 888-7777.

10. **People's Food Project:** We need people to telephone restaurants, food brokers and grocery stores to donate food to be distributed to churches and soup kitchens to help feed the poor and homeless. Call Joe at 345-6789.

11. Volunteers needed to man the **Smoker's Quitline.** Call 454-8995.

12. **Hospital Gift Shop** needs volunteers to sell gift items and cashier from 1 to 4 any afternoon. Call St. Joseph's Hospital 333-7777.

13. **Animal Rescue Center** needs volunteer to help put out weekly newspaper whose goal is to help pets find their owners, encourage people to adopt pets and provide information about the care and training of pets. Call Animals: 412-5123.

14. **Community Center** offering many courses day and evening needs volunteer to answer calls about their course offerings. Call 987-6543.

15. **Non-Profit Agency** which provides family planning information to schools and organizations needs someone to help with clerical work and bookkeeping. Call 256-4789.

Volunteer Coordinator	Date
Volunteer	**Organization & Reason for Suggestion**
#1	
#2	
#3	
#4	
#5	
#6	
#7	
#8	

The Projects

A *choice of communicative activities*

Choose one of the following projects. You may work alone or with one or two classmates.

Project One

Interview five people who have at one time or another worked as a volunteer. Find out what they did, how they got to do it, what they gained from doing it, and anything else that you think may be relevant. Take notes and report back to the class.

Project Two

Get information. "Let your fingers do the walking." In most phone books under "Social Service Organizations" or under "Volunteer Organizations" you will see a list of agencies, many of which are staffed by volunteers. From the list, find three agencies that are of interest to you, call them, and inquire about what kind of volunteer help they need.

Project Three

Find someone who is working as a volunteer now. Prepare a list of suitable questions and interview the person about his or her role as a volunteer.

Project Four

Where can you learn about volunteer jobs? Find out what departments in the university match volunteer students to jobs that need doing. Think of all the places where you can obtain such information.

Project Five

Call a local hospital. You will probably find an office for volunteers. Call them and find out what jobs people do in a hospital when they volunteer.

Project Six

Read the article "'Guiding spirit' answers rings, pulls strings" from the Boston Globe. Although Evelyn Nauyokas isn't a volunteer, her job is similar to Helen Chandler's job. Discuss what she does with the class and prepare a short vocabulary lesson for the class on some of the idiomatic expressions used in the article. Here are some idioms you may be interrested in: (You may have to consult native speakers since some of these may not be in your dictionary.)

to pull strings	putting all our heads together
hot line	on their toes
All the big shots think they can hide.	to tide them over
street sense	to stiff the company
cranks	mixed blessing
We don't have to look outside to know it's a full moon.	they're stranded

'Guiding spirit' answers rings, pulls strings

City Hall hot line operator is a problem-solver

By Joe Ferson
Contributing Reporter

The bank of telephones rings constantly inside Boston's City Hall—seven days a week, 24 hours a day—with most callers demanding, "Let me talk to the Mayor!"

Instead of Ray Flynn, callers often find themselves talking to Evelyn Nauyokas, who sits at one of the cluster of desks outside the mayor's office on the fifth floor. Leaning forward heavily on her elbows, chain-smoking and scrawling notes, she recently took a call from Jamaica Plain.

A sidewalk and street are strewn with garbage, she was told. Nauyokas notified the nearest Department of Public Works crew, and told the crew she expected immediate results.

"If you continue to have the problem, get back to us," she instructed the caller.

Nauyokas, who is one of 18 operators at the City Hall hot line, is known among co-workers as its "guiding spirit." They say she has an uncanny ability to solve problems and sooth complaints from sometimes frustrated, sometimes angry constituents.

"My Rolodex is right here," she said, pointing to her head. "You waste time if you have to look up a number."

If a problem persists, Nauyokas goes right to the top. "I'm not impressed by titles," she added.

Run by the Office of Neighborhood Services, the 24-hour hot line responds to complaints from city residents.

Another hot line operator, Robert Jenkins, vouches for his colleague's chutzpah. "She says and does things nobody else is capable of. She's unbelievable."

As an example, Nauyokas called the director of Inspectional Services, Peter Welsh, on a Sunday afternoon in late July.

Welsh was alerted when the residents of 63 Washington St. discovered that they were without electricity and their building was flooded.

"I love weekends," Nauyokas said. "All the big shots think they can hide."

The hot line operators know that department heads and neighborhood representatives carry beepers.

Nauyokas added, "You have to have a street sense, a judgment . . . there are a number of cranks who call."

Included in that group is a resident of East Boston who is convinced airplanes are dumping excessive fumes on the house, or the resident of Roslindale who complains of poisoned drinking water.

Both complaints have been investigated and found to be baseless, she said.

Instead, Nauyokas blames the heavens. "We don't have to look outside to know it's a full moon." she said.

Charlestown resident Leo Boucher, a former employee for the Department of Correction, has been answering calls at different hours of the day

Illus. based on Globe staff photo by Janet Knoff

Evelyn Nauyokas "says and does things nobody else is capable of," says one of her hot line coworkers.

for 18 months. He believes that most people who call — especially at night — are angry about something.

"Putting all our heads together we manage to get something done." Boucher said. "But Evelyn has a way of dealing with calls and the other departments. She's not afraid to say what she feels and people respond to that."

Jenkins, a resident of Mattapan who was hired three months ago, said, "She keeps everyone here loose, but at the same time, on their toes."

Besides rattling city officials, Nauyokas targets anyone who she thinks might be responsible.

"Landlords think twice about shutting off the power or heat, if they know we're on to them, She said.

In the event of an emergency during the winter, she said she pulls every string she has.

"I have a good relationship with the oil dealers. I tell the deliverer, 'Can you just let so-and-so have 50 gallons to tide them over for the weekend,' and I've never had anyone who called turn around and stiff the company," she said. "They always pay the bill."

Nauyokas added, "It never entered my mind that I was part of the system . . . I love this job, especially when I get the electricity turned on in a house where there's children or an elderly person."

Recently, she said, a caller showed up and introduced himself. "I try to imagine what the other person looks like, but I'm usually wrong," Nauyokas said.

"All along I pictured this shrunken and gray old man on the other end, and it turns out he was about six feet tall, stocky, and a nice looking man," she said. raising her eyebrows in surprise.

Married for 49 years, Nauyokas has lived all her life in South Boston, as have both her children. At home she keeps the police radio

squawking.

"I like to know what's going on in the city," she said. "My grandchildren think I'm crazy," she added with a touch of pride.

Her hometown fame, however, has been a mixed blessing.

"Whenever there's a power outage in South Boston, they say, 'Oh, give Evelyn a call, she'll fix it.'"

In addition to calling 725-4500, anyone can walk into city hall with a complaint and take it to the operators Monday through Friday 8:30 a.m. to 5 p.m.

An average of 250 calls are received each day by the hot line, according to supervisor Gerry Cuddyer.

Originally on the first floor, the hot line was moved to outside the mayor's office after Flynn became mayor.

On occasion, Flynn will walk by and answer calls, according to Nauyokas. "When he takes a call, the person on the other end is usually dumbfounded that they've managed to reach him." Nauyokas said.

Nauyokas speaks Lithuanian, a language she has had to use on the hot line. Other operators speak Spanish, Chinese, Haitian, Vietnamese and Cambodian. Mostly, the telephone operators use English to coordinate, patch, replace, respond or somehow deliver a service. Sometimes listening is all that is required.

Nauyokas used to be a nurse and thinks both jobs require compassion. "You have to sympathize with some people," she said. "They're stranded or they don't have power."

At 64, Nauyokas said: "I have to laugh when someone says, 'You don't know what it's like to be old.' I say, 'Oh, yes I do!' But, I'm not going to retire," she added quickly. "I'm staying right here."

Reprinted courtesy of The Boston Globe.

Lesson 7: Sam Adams, industrial engineer

Introductory Reading

When he was a student in high school, Sam Adams always liked and did well in his mathematics and science courses. As he thought about his future work he wavered between a career in medicine and a career in engineering, but by the time he entered Northeastern University in Boston, he had finally decided on engineering.

Sam enrolled in the School of Engineering and took courses in physics and chemistry and mathematics, along with introductory engineering and liberal arts courses, economics and Greek philosophy.

In his sophomore year, about the same time that he discovered that he was more concerned with people than he was with producing a product—such as a road, a bridge, a house or a factory—he discovered the field of industrial engineering, and he knew he had found what he wanted to study and to do.

Most industrial engineers are employed by manufacturing industries, but their training and skills are useful in a variety of workplaces including hospitals, banks, large and small businesses, and insurance companies. Does that seem strange? What is an engineer doing working in a small business . . . or a hospital . . . ? After you have heard Sam you should be able to understand.

What exactly is an industrial engineer, and what does an I.E. do? From your cassette tape, as Sam tells you about his first job as a hired consultant in the field, you will get a picture of the work in this profession. He is going to tell you why he was attracted to this work and finally, before you finish this chapter, he is going to admit to you why he wasn't a complete success in his first assignment. ◢

Work Related Vocabulary

These words or phrases are used in the interview you're about to hear. In groups discuss the vocabulary, sharing knowledge and using a dictionary when needed. Check (✓) off those words you already know. If a word or phrase is new to you and you want to learn it, in the space beside it either write its meaning in English or in your own language or write an English sentence using it.

1. an efficiency expert
2. a payroll
3. a union
4. non-union
5. labor
6. a short-term basis
7. a consultant
8. quality control
9. a product
10. to go on strike
11. an assembly line
12. work flow
13. a minimum wage

Additional vocabulary

1. a slob
2. hammers, saws, nails
3. kitchen utensils
4. monotony
5. boredom

 # The Interview

Tape: Part One—The first listening 1

Listen to the interview trying to get a general understanding, the gist, of what the discussion is about and then answer the following questions:

Questions

1. What did you learn about Sam and his work in this first listening?

2. What are the most interesting things you learned about Sam and his work?

3. Did anything you learned from the interview surprise you?

 # Vocabulary in Context

Tape: Part Two—Listening exercise 2

Listen to the recording and write down the word or phrase you hear. You will hear the word or phrase twice. Then, listen to two sentences in which that word or phrase is used. (The second sentence is taken from the conversation you have heard.) Next, write down what you think that word or phrase means. Make an intelligent guess, using context clues.

1. Listen and write: _____
   Meaning:

2. Listen and write: _____
   Meaning:

3. Listen and write: _____
   Meaning:

4. Listen and write: _____
   Meaning:

5. Listen and write: _____
   Meaning:

6. Listen and write: _____
   Meaning:

Now that you have done the vocabulary in context, listen to the interview again.

The Interview

Reconstruction

All of the following words or phrases appear, chronologically, in the interview. Working with a partner, tell something interesting or significant about the word or phrase, as it relates to the interview. For example: "some sort of book." Possible reconstruction: "He's doing the interview for some sort of book." "Who is?" "The interviewer."

1. microphone
2. taped interviews
3. well-organized and neat
4. socks and underwear
5. a real slob
6. kitchen utensils
7. flip side—bossy
8. Mr. Hobbs
9. non-union
10. quality control
11. lunch break
12. absentminded

The Interview concludes

Now listen to the recommendations that Sam Adams made. How do they compare to the recommendations you made? Were there any differences?

 # The Dialogue

 3

Tape: Part Three—Sam and Jane

Listen to this conversation. Answer the following questions:

Questions

1. Are you surprised by what Sam had learned about the factory? What is your opinion of Mr. Hobbs, the owner?

2. At the very end, what does he mean by "One step forward and two steps backward"?

The Interactive Listening

 4

Tape: Part Four—Three riddles

Industrial engineers must be good listeners; they must be intelligent, observant, and able to solve problems. On this part of the tape you will hear three unusual riddles. Listen carefully. Can you solve them? Explain your solutions in writing below on this page.

1.

2.

3.

The Projects

A *choice of communicative activities*

Choose one of the following projects. You may work alone or with one or two classmates.

Project One

Analyze the information and vocabulary in "Help Wanted" advertisements. Study this sample advertisement from *L. L. Bean* and the information taken from it and recorded in the grid below. Then choose one of the ads given on the next page and another from your local newspaper. Be sure the one you find advertises a job which someone with a degree in industrial engineering could apply for. On the next page are two blank grids. Analyze the ads you have chosen and fill out the grids. When you are finished, share your grids and new vocabulary with your classmates.

L. L. Bean®
Professional Opportunties in the Maine Tradition.
QUALITY ASSURANCE SUPERVISOR

Responsibilities will include the development of product quality standards and their communication to our vendors. Training of internal quality inspectors will also be included as well as supervision of support staff.

The successful candidate will have a college degree and minimum of 3 years manufacturing experience in a textile or apparel industry, with focus on product quality. Travel will be required. Proven ability to communicate at all levels within an organization is necessary. Individual must be a self starter with good organizational skills. Supervisory experience preferred.

L.L. Bean provides a competitive compensation and benefits package. To explore this opportunity, please send your resume with cover letter indicating position desired and salary requirements to: Martha Kidd Cyr, Staffing Manager, L.L. Bean, Inc., Casco Street, Freeport, ME 04033.

We Are An Equal Opportunity Employer
Courtesy L.L. Bean, Inc.

Information from the sample ad:

Position: *Quality Assurance Supervisor*

Firm: *L. L. Bean*

Requirements — Degree: *Not specified*

Specific Experience: *3 years in manufacturing environment — textile or apparel supervisory experience preferred*

Special Knowledge: *How to develop product quality standards*
How to train internal quality inspectors
How to supervise support staff

Personal Qualities: *Ability to communicate at all levels*
Self-starter
Good organizational skills

Special Requirements: *Willingness to travel*

Benefits — Salary: *Not stated*

Fringe Benefits: *Not explained*

To apply send: *1. Resumé*
2. Cover letter which should include the position wanted and salary

New Vocabulary: *vendors, support staff, apparel, self-starter, benefits package, equal opportunity employer*

Technical Consultants

Put your manufacturing and/or financial background to work at TRY Computer. As the leading independent vendor of software for manufacturing companies in the U.S., we know that our customers are our most important asset. That's why our technical consultants are people who understand manufacturing. Professionals our customers can rely on to help answer their technical and applications questions, solve systems problems, and provide them with new product information and training.

As a technical consultant based in our Burlington office, you'll support our response center using the TRY accounting and manufacturing software and convert new customers while lending technical support to our staff.

The position requires 1-3 years in a manufacturing environment with VAX, VMS, DBMS and/or HP 3000 experience. FORTRAN experience a plus. A degree in Computer Science, Business or equivalent is desirable.

We offer you a competitive compensation package including cash profit sharing, 401(k), and stock purchase plans. For immediate consideration, send your resume with salary history to Customer Support Manager, TRY Computer Systems Inc., 14 Pilgrim Executive Park, Athol, MA 01803. EOE, m/f/h/v.

TRY

SYSTEMS ENGINEERING

Expanding professional and technical service firm expects to have opening for qualified acquisition task managers and system engineers to support USAF electronic systems acquisition. We require mature self-starting professionals with the following minimum qualifications:

- B.S. Degree or better in a scientific/engineering discipline or business. Hands on experience in system acquisition, preferably of Air Force elec. sys./c31 programs.
- Minimum 3 years experience in system engineering and AFSC acquisition policies.
- Knowledge of logistics engineering and configuration management to include logistics support analysis, life cycle cost analysis and integrated logistics support is desirable. Demonstrable technical writing skills and speaking ability required.

Primary work location within 15 miles of Hanscom AFB. Those who meet requirements, please forward your resume with specific salary requirements to:

P.O. Box #564
Potter Square
Harvard, MA 02155

An affirmative Action/Equal Opportunity Employer

LIFE-LAB

Put Your Experience To The Test.

Challenge—you'll find it at Digitex. If you have the ambition and experience to pursue our leading electronics and optics technologies, you'll score positive career results.

QUALITY CONTROL TECHNICIAN

Responsible for testing and troubleshooting a wide variety of computer subassemblies and peripherals. You should have a firm background in basic electronics and ability to understand system to component levels. Individual must be able to work independently and interface easily with other people.

Here, in a professional, yet informal, environment, you'll enjoy a highly competitive salary, and outstanding benefits, including 100% tuition reimbursement, flexible hours and free parking. **For prompt attention, forward your resume and salary history, in confidence, to: Patricia B. DiMilano, Life-Lab Incorporated, Digitex Research, 246 MIT Avenue, Harvard, MA 02154.**

Digitex Research

INDUSTRIAL ENGINEER

Oakdale Sensors, Inc. a leading world supplier of thermal sensors, serving data processing, telecommunicators, military and aerospace markets, has a need for an industrial engineer in the Precision Division.

Responsibilities involve classical I.E. functions with emphasis on process and methods improvements. JLT, equipment evaluations and cost reductions. The successful candidate will have demonstrated ability to contribute to a fast-paced, results-oriented environment.

A BSIE degree or equivalent, with 3-5 years' experience, is required.

At Elmwood you'll enjoy a very competitive salary with benefits including medical/dental/life disability insurance, educational reimbursement. 401K plan and more...

If you feel qualified, please send your resume with salary history to:
Jayne Serpente
Personnel Department

Oakdale Sensors Inc.

400 Narragansett Bay Place
Providence, RI 02861
An Equal Opportunity Employer M/F/V/H

CONTRACT POSITIONS in Computer Applications and Quality Control

If you're computer literate and would like to learn more about interactive video, consider these contract positions: we'll train you to use our software and computer-based training, to "Author" our programs using flowcharts and specifications created by our project designers. You'll also be responsible for maintaining and evaluating documentation provided by design teams, editing and performing quality control on interactive video programs, and modifying these programs to meet Spectrum Interactive's design standards.

If you have data entry, word processing or other computer related experience in your background, excellent organizational and communication skills, and the proven ability to work independently, this is an excellent opportunity! Familiarity with a programming language is beneficial but not necessary.

We're located just off Essex Turnpike at 9 Elm Park Drive, Dorchester, MA 01764. Please send your resume and salary requirements to J. Billings. We're an Equal Opportunity Employer M/F.

RAINBOW REACTIONS

Exeter

Exeter Healthcare Corporation, a Fortune 100 company and developer and manufacturer of diagnostic test kits, has an immediate opportunity for a:

Manufacturing Engineer
Position involves the management and development of projects to improve the manufacturing process and to reduce costs. Projects range from package redesign to systems development. Requirements include a BS in Engineering or equivalent. Industrial engineering concentration preferred. A Master's or MBA would be a plus. 1-2 years experience preferred.

Exeter offers a competitive salary and an excellent benefits package. Please send your resume in confidence to Mona DeFlamme White, 800 Memorial Drive, Cambridge, MA 02154.

An equal opportunity/affirmative action employer.

Information from an ad on the previous page:

Information from your newspaper ad:

Position:	**Position:**
Firm:	**Firm:**

Requirements — Degree:	**Requirements** — Degree:
Specific Experience:	Specific Experience:
Special Knowledge:	Special Knowledge:
Personal Qualities:	Personal Qualities:
Special Requirements:	Special Requirements:

Benefits — Salary:	**Benefits** — Salary:
Fringe Benefits:	Fringe Benefits:
To apply, send:	To apply, send:

New Vocabulary:	**New Vocabulary:**

Project Two

Find out where you can get a degree in industrial engineering in your area. Read university brochures in your library or a counselor's office and/or visit a local university's admission office. Make notes on what you learn on the grid; an example based on a brochure and an interview has been done for you.

Northeastern University Boston, Massachusetts offers Master of Science degrees in Engineering Management Industrial Engineering

MSEM. There is a constantly growing need for technically qualified engineering managers: men and women who are not only technically qualified, but who can motivate, lead and manage people in today's complex business environment.

The master's degree program in Engineering Management helps facilitate the transition into management. The MSEM Program differs from the MBA Program, because it is designed for engineers and scientists and, as such, presumes a solid quantitative background upon which to build management within a technical environment.

The **MSEM** helps to ease the transition from purely technical professional to first level manager; its focus is on management within a technical environment.

MSIE. Industrial Engineering is the engineering discipline in which the human components of systems in problem analysis and solution are addressed. One definition speaks of the integration of people, materials, machinery and money. To accomplish this goal, a competent industrial engineer must master a wide variety of tools and techniques and have a thorough understanding of the human component.

Industrial engineers provide the solution to complex, multi-faceted manufacturing or service delivery problems. A single problem may require the use of computers and information systems, man-machine interface, statistical analysis and optimization. The graduate program in Industrial Engineering provides this requisite diversity of skills.

University: *Northeastern*

Degree received:

Master of Science in Engineering Management or Industrial Engineering

Entering qualifications or admissions requirements:

B. Sc. Acceptable undergrad record or possibly a degree in math or science. Proficiency in probability statistics, human factors, accounting, engineering, economics, operations research, computer programing.

Time involved

Is it part time or full time? The brochure does not say.

Possible courses

*Organizational psychology
Simulation methodology
Applied statistics
Advanced operations research*

Advantages — skills — jobs

I will learn how to integrate people, materials, machinery and money.

I may get to work for an important company (Polaroid, etc.), even become a president, vice-president, or senior manager.

University:

Degree received:

Entering qualifications or admissions requirements:

Time involved

Possible courses

Advantages — skills — jobs

Project Three

Interview an industrial engineer. Plan your questions so that you find out about his background, his job, and other things you want to know.

Project Four

Interview an industrial engineering student. Plan your questions so that you find out about the courses he is taking, any experience he has had, the kind of job he hopes to be doing when he graduates, and any other things you want to know.

Project Five

Try your listening skills as if you were an industrial engineer. Ask someone in an office, a shop, or even at home to tell you about some procedure they follow which is a problem for them. Ask them if they have any ideas to make the procedure easier. If you have any suggestions to make, make them. Then report on your experience to your class.

Project Six

Read about three industrial engineers in the following selection. Report to the class on the jobs each industrial engineer does, and prepare a list of vocabulary to teach to your classmates.

INDUSTRIAL ENGINEERS TALK ABOUT THEIR WORK

Industrial Engineer A

Why are we getting so many returns of our chain saws?

This was the question thrown at me in production management meeting.

I'm the head industrial engineer of this large diversified manufacturer of small power equipment and tools. I have a large staff of IEs under me. There are from two to five IEs in each of the seven production plants (located nationwide) operated by this manufacturer. Our jobs are closely related with the Mechanical Engineers who design our tools.

My education was Industrial Engineering with added courses in Mechanical Engineering.

Returns of products from customers because of malfunction are very costly, and our reputation for quality products is hurt.

Complaints started coming in from our company distribution centers, and from jobbers and wholesalers. Returns of our #16 inch gasoline chain saw were coming from hardware stores, garden stores, machinery jobbers, and from large direct buyers, utility companies, lumber companies, and tree maintenance companies.

I called in the head of our mechanical enginering department, the head of production, and several line machine operators.

We put several of our #16's on a bench. The notations of complaints from our district offices read:

"Starting is difficult."

"Starter rope broke."

"Starter rope came off the second time I pulled it."

There were other complaints, but nearly all were about the rope pull.

"How long have these complaints been coming in? It has taken about two months for complaints to filter into headquarters."

Records showed customers were given a new saw. Records showed that several of the replacement saws had trouble.

"What happened two months ago in production?" I asked the production workers. I was brought records of changes on the production line. I saw there were new machines installed almost three months ago. These clamp a metal clip on the end of the starting rope, which catches, to keep the rope from being pulled out of the crank wind.

We went to the plant and to the machines; saw them in operation, examined the rope, examined

71

the clips. I pulled one of the clips off a rope with my screwdriver. The metal was too soft. I remembered recommending the purchase and installation of these machines, for more efficiency in production. Mechanical Engineering had tested the machines, clips and ropes. But this metal clip won't do.

Formerly we had machines that tied a small knot at the end of the rope, but an operator had to feed the rope through a small metal hole in the inner frame, a slow operation.

Back at the bench in my office we started taking the returned saws apart. Each was in its box, and there was the loose rope. The loose clip on one was bent and caught in the edge of the cranking shaft. I got it loose.

I got a copy of the "Operations Sheet" enclosed with each saw. Starting procedures were completely explained and there was a caution not to pull the cranking rope all the way. Short pulls are adequate to start.

Customers must not be reading this sheet—or maybe they can't read English.

My directions: Print our operations sheet in several languages. Order better quality metal clips and test. Recall all units from distributors. Reinstitute tying knot in rope until we get better clips.

Some of my work is not strictly Industrial Engineering which is designing and testing systems of production and labor. However, in my case I am in an upper echelon position as head IE. I am next to management.

Industrial Engineer B

Officers of the life insurance company I work for have shared the concern of government and private industry about inflation, recession, energy problems, and decline in trade. They read the reports on lack of productivity growth, agreeing that workers cannot produce well using obsolescent machinery and that the U.S. has invested less of its wealth in updating factories and equipment than have other industrial nations. They observed that oil, chemical, paper, electronics, and other production industries were adding to their management teams people with the new title of productivity managers. Concluding that a service business might similarly benefit, they installed me as productivity manager, with a broad mandate.

The first studies we began are on more efficient uses of equipment and energy. We are looking into costs of health and antipollution measures. We are preparing alternatives on where to invest if tax cuts occur. We are studying developments in technological systems. We are collecting data on jobs where productivity is especially low. We are doing research on quality of working life.

In this new field I work under the direct supervision of the president of the company. We are concerned not with short-term answers but with long-range planning.

Industrial Engineer C

Sometimes it seems as if IEs are blamed by workers for every change that comes to a plant. In my case I experienced something else. It's true that in this small paint factory I've been pretty unpopular at times when jobs have been changed because we brought in more standardized components and several kinds of automation. I gained points when my study of an excessive number of component rejects in one operation showed that it was the machine and not the workers causing the trouble. Another machine was designed for 6-footers. The operations caused fatigue and irritation when run by shorter operators. I had the machine legs shortened; the correction saved money and tempers.

About three years ago the corporate owner gave up the battle for profits, and it looked very much as though there would either be extensive layoffs or the plant would close. At a union meeting, members considered the possibility of buying the company, and I was asked for advice and then offered advancement from IE to general manager. I knew we needed capital for some very necessary equipment. I did a feasibility study, on the strength of which we obtained a government loan. The transition took time; I had to convince workers that to continue low productivity of the past would be fatal and that changes were inevitable.

In this type of factory the start-up costs at the beginning of the day are heavy; so I altered the production lines for more efficiency. After some initial opposition, attitudes changed. Production increased and began to keep up with orders.

This is not a total success story—we still face many problems. But our sales have increased, and workers take very seriously their contribution to decision making. Meanwhile no jobs have been lost, and the community hasn't suffered from a closed plant. Owner-Management is satisfied and there is talk about buying some new machinery.

Credit: The Institute for Research Northfield, Illinois

Project Seven

Read the following short selection. Then ask five people what they think good listening involves. Take notes. Also ask them what jobs they think require attentive listening skills. Organize your notes and report to the class on the reading and the interviews.

Learning to Speak the Native Tongue.

I was twenty-two and fresh out of college when I got my first job as a production foreman in a linen mill. Needless to say, I was eager to put my skills to work for me and to prove myself as a manager. Unfortunately, I was so eager that I began to talk *at* and not *to* my new staff, made up entirely of middle-aged women.

As is the case in many offices and factories, seniority meant clout in my sewing room, so when my first set of directives was prepared, I made sure I presented them to the woman who had been there long enough to make an imposing impression on her peers—a woman known as Big Helen.

She greeted me as soon as I approached her. "Hello, Kevin," she said. I was pleased—here was a woman who seemed genuinely to welcome my input despite the thirty-year gap in our ages! Encouraged, I began to outline my decisions about the way the sewing room had to be run. "Okay, Kevin!" she answered, and hurried back to her station, I *thought,* to put my insights into operation. Yet, by that afternoon, it was business as usual—and I decided to speak to Big Helen again.

I never asked Helen for her input. I never asked whether she had any questions that might have prevented her from implementing my suggestions. Instead, I reiterated my plans for reorganizing the sewing room. "Okay, Kevin!" said Big Helen, who turned on her heel and headed straight back to her station.

Shortly thereafter, I saw Helen in conversation with her co-workers, which I took as a good sign. Yet, by the next morning the sewing room was going full force, and none of my suggestions had been taken. By noon I had sought the advice of the previous production foreman.

"I think I'm having a little personnel problem," I began. However, as I outlined my confrontation with Big Helen, his smile became harder to suppress.

"Well, what did you want Helen to do, Kevin?" he asked. I briefed him on my plan.

"Then we'd better go tell her in Polish because the only words of English she knows are 'Hello, Kevin' and 'Okay, Kevin.'"

No doubt about it, my nerves and eagerness had gotten the better of me. But although my managerial "deafness" was pointed up by my inability to perceive even the most basic data about my employees, talking too much too often has the same effect in *any* language.

Introductory Reading

Your main challenge while listening to this interview with Rebecca Kraus is going to be to try to keep up with and keep track of all the unpredictable changes that Rebecca has made in her career over the years.

There was a time in the history of the United States when most everyone entered a job and stayed with that work through his or her working life. Today it is not unusual for a person to change careers two, three or more times during a lifetime.

Examples: the forty-five year-old newspaper editor who receives what he considers to be a religious calling and gives up all to prepare to become an Episcopalian priest; the twenty-seven year-old English teacher who decides she wants to make a lot of money and goes off to get a master's degree in business administration (MBA) so that she can become an upwardly mobile business executive; the successful fifty-five year-old banker who decides to buy a small inn in Vermont in order to do what he has always wanted to do—become a gourmet cook and manager of a small business.

This happens all the time in the United States these days.

The belief that "variety is the very spice of life that gives it all its flavour" (Cowper) is one of the motivations for the desire for change. Another motivation is that some people fear that, if they get bored with their work, they will become boring people.

Rebecca's case is slightly different. She considers herself tuned in to some inner voice which continues to call her to be open for change. Basically, she is proud of that attitude. Listen to how her life undergoes those small changes slowly, almost imperceptibly. But change she does, until, finally, you'll hardly recognize her. ঌ

Work Related Vocabulary

These words or phrases are used in the interview you're about to hear. In groups discuss the vocabulary, sharing knowledge and using a dictionary when needed. Check (✓) off those words you already know. If a word or phrase is new to you and you want to learn it, in the space beside it either write its meaning in English or in your own language or write an English sentence using it.

1. tubes and circuits
2. vacuum tubes
3. (computer) software
4. (computer) hardware
5. systems engineering
6. digital processing
7. a systems analyst
8. civil engineering
9. contraction theories
10. stress
11. reinforced concrete
12. elasticity
13. a teaching assistant
14. tuition
15. curriculum work
16. transfer students

Additional vocabulary

1. a rumbling sound
2. music conservatory
3. to plunge into
4. apoplectic
5. a loony bin
6. absurd
7. conceited
8. obstinate
9. to delve into

The Interview

 1

Tape: Part One—The first listening

Listen to the interview trying to get a general understanding, the gist, of what the discussion is about and then answer the following questions:

Questions

1. What did you learn about Rebecca and her work in this first listening?

2. What are the most interesting things you learned about Rebecca and her work?

3. Did anything you learned from the interview surprise you?

Vocabulary in Context

 2

Tape: Part Two—Listening exercise

Listen to the recording and write down the word or phrase you hear. You will hear the word or phrase twice. Then, listen to two sentences in which that word or phrase is used. (The second sentence is taken from the conversation you have heard.) Next, write down what you think that word or phrase means. Make an intelligent guess, using context clues.

1. Listen and write: _____
   Meaning:
2. Listen and write: _____
   Meaning:
3. Listen and write: _____
   Meaning:
4. Listen and write: _____
   Meaning:
5. Listen and write: _____
   Meaning:
6. Listen and write: _____
   Meaning:

Now that you have done the vocabulary in context, listen to the interview again.

The Interview

Tape: Part One, again—The second listening   1

Reconstruction

Working with a partner, comment on each of the following phrases that you heard in the interview. Give the context for the phrase and explain as fully as possible what the person was talking about.

1. Mozart
2. a little vacuum tube
3. "The Last Rose of Summer"
4. a music conservatory
5. Georgia Tech
6. software and hardware
7. apoplectic
8. a loony bin
9. John
10. raising a roof
11. master's degree
12. teaching assistant
13. assistant dean
14. international students
15. Mozart

 # The Dialogue

Tape: Part Three — Rebecca and Budi Winotta   3

Listen to this conversation. Answer the following questions:

Questions

1. Why can Rebecca understand the student's dilemma so well?

2. What are the similarities and differences in Rebecca's career and the student's future career?

3. Rebecca's story suggests that many things influence what people do and become in their working lives and that the paths we expect to follow when we are eighteen often change in surprising ways. Discuss this.

The Interactive Listening

 4

Tape: Part Four—A listening comprehension test

This is a multiple choice test. It is similar in construction to the listening section of the Michigan Test or the TOEFL test except that all the information is about engineers and engineering. The information has been taken from the Occupational Outlook Handbook 1988-1989 Edition *published by U.S. Department of Labor and Bureau of Labor Statistics. Listen carefully to the statement on the tape. Choose one of the three statements, a, b, or c, that is closest to what you have heard. Mark your answers on the answer sheet in your student's book on page 81.*

1. a. There will be fewer metalurgical, ceramic, and materials engineers by the year 2000.
    b. Jobs for metalurgical, ceramic, and materials engineers are expected to increase in the next ten years.
    c. There will be more metalurgical, ceramic, and materials engineers than any other kinds of engineers by the year 2000.

2. a. We are expecting a large increase in the number of mining engineers by the year 2000 because the world is expected to need an increased supply of minerals.
    b. Most mining engineers are very level-headed.
    c. The number of mining engineers will probably remain about the same until the end of the century.

3. a. Almost 200,000 civil engineers were employed by the U.S. government in 1986.
    b. Government agencies employed less than 100,000 civil engineers in the year 1986.
    c. Very few civil engineers work for the government.

4. a. Even with advanced methods, petroleum engineers only get 50% of the oil in a reservoir.
    b. The petroleum engineer recovers almost all of the oil out of the reservoir.
    c. Petroleum engineers are fully satisfied with the methods they are now using to extract oil from petroleum reservoirs.

5. a. There are expected to be a lot of job opportunities for nuclear engineers because there is expected to be a great deal of growth in these areas.
    b. Graduate programs in nuclear engineering are turning out many new graduates with degrees in this field.
    c. There are not many people who have degrees in nuclear engineering.

6. a. There is not much point in getting a bachelor's degree in engineering.
    b. You can teach in an accredited engineering program if you have a bachelor's degree in engineering.
    c. You can find a job in engineering if you have a bachelor's degree in engineering.

7. a. Starting engineers make little more money than starting graduates with other degrees.
    b. Starting engineers make a lot more money than starting graduates with other degrees.
    c. Starting engineers make a little more money than starting graduates with other degrees.

8. a. Electrical engineers are rarely employed by the defense industry.
    b. If less money is spent on the nation's defense, some electrical engineers will be fired.
    c. If we spend more money on defense, we will cut back on electrical engineers.

9. a. Once you have a Ph.D in engineering, it is not necessary to learn anymore.
    b. The things that engineers need to know remains constant.
    c. Because information changes rapidly, engineers must stay up-to-date.

10. a. Engineers usually work alone and don't need to be very sociable.
    b. Engineers should be able to both speak and write well the language of the country in which they are working.
    c. If an engineer is creative, he or she doesn't have to bother with detail.

Answer Sheet

Mark the spaces below which correspond to the numbers of the statements which most nearly resemble the statements you hear on the tape.

	a	b	c		a	b	c		a	b	c
1.	○	○	○	5.	○	○	○	9.	○	○	○
2.	○	○	○	6.	○	○	○	10.	○	○	○
3.	○	●	○	7.	○	○	○				
4.	○	○	○	8.	○	○	⊗				

The Projects

A *choice of communicative activities*

Choose one of the following projects. You may work alone or with one or two classmates.

Project One

Ask five people how they learned to do the jobs they do. You will need to get the following information. What do they do in their job? Did they learn to do what they do in grade school, high school, or college? Did they go through a trade school or special training program? Did they learn on the job? How important to their work has their formal academic education been? Has their academic education been important to them in other ways? Report your findings to your class.

Project Two

Survey people's attitudes about various career patterns. Design questions asking people's opinions on such issues as: whether people should change jobs to get more money or responsibility from another company in the same field of work; whether they should stay loyally with one company; whether they should change to different fields as their interrests change; what jobs are appropriate for men or women, for older people, for youngsters just out of school; whether people should retire and when; or how people's attitudes about careers have changed over time.

When you have your questions, choose two contrasting groups of people to survey. You might choose "blue collar" and "white collar" workers; men and women; students and young people who are working; people in their twenties or thirties and elderly (even retired) people; or native-born Americans and people who have come from other countries.

Break up into two or more groups to do the survey. Each group should organize the information it collects and then present it to the rest of the class. Finally, compare the findings of your different groups and describe what you have learned.

Project Three

Find out how people use their "spare time." Many people, like Dean Kraus, have personal callings or avocations as well as their regular employment or vocations. They may be serious, though not professional, artists: painters, sculptors, musicians, poets, or novelists. They may have other kinds of hobbies which take a lot of time and which they take very seriously. Design a survey to discover how people spend their spare time and to discover how this varies between cultures or depending on people's financial or educational backgrounds. Share what you learn in a class discussion.

The following projects all relate to engineering. If you are studying at a university or have access to a university, these projects offer some interesting ways to learn about it.

Project Four

Working in groups, you will learn about the position of women like Rebecca Kraus in the field of engineering and in engineering schools. This project requires four students or four groups. Each group goes separately to a different engineering school to get the following information:

Group 1 will find out what the ratio of male students is to female students in the department of electrical engineering.

Group 2 will find out what the ratio of male students is to female students in the department of computer engineering.

Group 3 will find out what the ratio of male students is to female students in the department of mechanical engineering.

Group 4 will find out what the ratio of male students is to female students in the department of civil engineering.

After the data is collected, fill in the following chart. Discuss the data.

Name of the University: _____ Date: _____			
Department	Number of men enrolled	Number of women enrolled	Ratio M/W
Electrical Engineering			
Computer Engineering			
Mechanical Engineering			
Civil Engineering			
Engineering School totals			

Questions to Discuss:

A. Did you get the data you expected?

   If the ratio is not 50/50, what reasons do you think there are for the differences?

   What do you think the ratio is in other countries?

B. Read the article "Some colleges work to attract women into engineering."

   How does the data mentioned in the article compare with your data?

   What reasons are given in the article for the decline in the number of women in the engineering field?

Some colleges work to attract women into engineering

By Sandra Sokoloff
Special to the Globe

Elizabeth Ivey, professor of physics and chairwoman of the physics department at Smith College, remembers counseling two women engineering students. "They were both in tears," recalls Ivey. "Not because they were intimidated by the workload, but because a professor in another school was constantly giving them a difficult time in class. Eventually, one of the women ended up dropping the course."

This event is not a memory of bygone days but a recent occurrence—and one example of what's pushing women away from engineering careers, according to educators.

Declining numbers of women entering engineering programs have propelled many private and public Massachusetts-based colleges and universities to seek new ways to draw women into the field of engineering. Educators, however, maintain that only when the field, schools and general society change their attitude and approach toward women will large numbers enter engineering.

According to Jane Daniels, director of the Women in Engineering Program at Purdue University in West Lafayette, Ind., who tracks national engineering enrolments, the growing decline of women in the field is particularly disappointing. "From 1970 to 1983, there was a great spurt of women entering engineering." she says. "Nationwide, engineering programs had 15 to 16 percent female students. Then, in 1983, things came to a screeching halt."

Ivey says that despite engineering's professional and personal opportunities, very few women ever seriously consider the field. "Young women contemplating future careers have far more complex adult identity issues, such as marriage and child-rearing, to deal with than young men their same age," says Ivey. She runs a summer workshop, "Current Students, Future Engineers," for high school science and math teachers and guidance counselors to help break down educational stereotypes that separate women from engineering.

Some educators agree with Frederick Nelson, dean of Tufts University's College of Engineering, who says, "There's not a decline in the number of women entering engineering, but in the number of students interested in this field. Today, many more careers compete for the attention of math and science-oriented students." But Ivey contends that the decline is not just demographic. "Subtle things happen to turn women away from engineering," says Ivey. "Often women don't get asked to do field work. In graduate school, they're often offered the lower-paying, less-significant teaching assistantships, rather than lab-oriented research assistantships."

Other educators cite a growing conservative trend and the lackluster momentum of the women's movement as national societal factors pushing women away from engineering. "In the late 1960s," says Daniels, "a sudden burst of social change coincided with decreasing engineering enrollments. Large corporations got nervous and began funding university programs to inform women about the field. Now that corporations see a few women in the industry, they think everything is fine. At Purdue, corporate funding for women in engineering programs has dropped 50 percent since 1979."

Meanwhile, at Tufts University, 185 women were enrolled in the College of Engineering for 1986-1987, as compared to the 221 total of 1984-1985. Robert Voss, executive director of admissions and financial aid at Worcester Polytechnic Institute, says, "In 1984, we had 132 freshmen women engineering students. In 1987, we only had 102." Boston University's College of Engineering is down to 22 percent female enrollment as opposed to the 24 percent figure of 1982 through 1985. Dr. Nancy Hellman, dean and director of the Women's Program in the College of Engineering at the University of Massachusetts at Amherst, admits that at UMass-Amherst a decline of the female engineering student by two-tenths of a percent is minuscule, but concedes that it does reflect the growing national trend.

"Right now, women comprise 13 percent of the college of engineering," says Paula Leventman, director of Northeastern University's Women in Engineering Program, "and we've really tread water to maintain this number." Some educators believe that state-supported schools with lower tuition rates, such as the University of Lowell and Southeastern Massachusetts University, and internationally recognized engineering programs such as MIT have an added buffer.

Institutions are trying a variety of methods to halt the shortage of female engineering students. Northeastern University has created a videotape to illustrate the intellectual challenges and rewards that engineering has to offer women. In addition, Northeastern has developed support services, study groups and networking opportunities for its women engineering students. UMass-Amherst female engineering students visit high schools and participate in the College of Engineering's career day to attract high school women to the field.

Women engineers are important to the field as well as to society, says Daniels. "We are a technologically based society," concludes Leventman. "Not to have half the population take advantage of growing professional opportunities is very disturbing and problematic."

Reprinted courtesy of Sandra Sokoloff.

Project Five

List for the class all the major fields of engineering and all the specialties. (e.g., biomedical engineering)

Project Six

Analyze the "Help Wanted Advertisements." What kinds of jobs are available for engineers? What kinds of education and experience are required? What are the salaries and benefits? Report to the class on your findings.

Project Seven

Interview an engineering student. Find out about the courses he or she is taking. See if the courses are theoretical or practical. What does he or she want to do when he or she graduates? etc. Report to the class on the interview.

Project Eight

Interview an engineer. If you do this in pairs, prepare your questions together. For example, you might ask: What kind of engineer are you? When did you decide you were going to be an engineer? What educaton did you need? Will you please tell us about your most recent project? After discussing the engineer's answers with your partner, tell the class about the interview.

Lesson 9: Tom Hyatt, medical intern

Introductory Reading

Tom Hyatt, whom you will meet in this chapter, is a medical intern in a hospital. It goes without saying that he has had to work and study very hard to get where he is; his education has been long and arduous, and it isn't finished yet.

When he graduated from high school, he entered Carleton College, a small college with a four year liberal arts program, in Northfield, Minnesota. He wasn't at all sure what he wanted to do with his life, but in college he became very interested in both biology and chemistry and began to think of medicine as a career possibility. During his junior (third) year he decided to become a doctor, and he applied to several medical schools. In his senior (fourth) year he was accepted at New York University.

Medical school is a four-year program, and during the first two years Tom took many courses in such things as anatomy, biology, and physiology. In the last two years in medical school, he spent a large proportion of his school time doing actual medical work, under the careful supervision of the hospital doctors in the New York University Hospital. During those two years, in order to obtain a broad understanding of all medical fields, he worked in a variety of medical specialties, including internal medicine, pediatrics, psychiatry, obstetrics, gynecology, and surgery. At that time he also did an independent study project in heart transplants.

After the four year program, Tom took his exams to qualify for his Medical Doctorship (M.D.) Then, having passed the exams and having received his M.D., he began a required three year residency at the hospital. The first year of residency is called internship. At this point—when we meet Tom in the taped interview—he is leaning toward a general practice of medicine (also called family practice) rather than specialization, so he has gone into the first year of a family practice residency.

It is not too late for him to change his mind and become a Specialist, but if he does so he will need to take three years of residency in the specialty he chooses.

Early in his intern year of residency Tom is working in the emergency ward of the hospital. ↄ

Work Related Vocabulary

These words or phrases are used in the interview you're about to hear. In groups discuss the vocabulary, sharing knowledge and using a dictionary when needed. Check (✓) off those words you already know. If a word or phrase is new to you and you want to learn it, in the space beside it either write its meaning in English or in your own language or write an English sentence using it.

1. a surgeon
2. surgery
3. a general practitioner
4. an emergency ward
5. to commit suicide
6. unconscious
7. a heart attack
8. an ambulance
9. an electrocardiograph
10. a massive coronary
11. intensive care
12. in shock
13. x-ray
14. pelvic
15. a dislocated shoulder
16. sprains
17. cuts
18. bruises
19. suture work
20. setting bones
21. stitches
22. a pediatrician
23. an obstetrician
24. a gynecologist

The Interview

 1

Tape: Part One—The first listening

Listen to the interview trying to get a general understanding, the gist, of what the discussion is about and then answer the following questions:

Questions

1. What did you learn about Tom and his work in this first listening?

2. What are the most interesting things you learned about Tom and his work?

3. Did anything you learned from the interview surprise you?

Vocabulary in Context

 2

Tape: Part Two—Listening exercise

Listen to the recording and write down the word or phrase you hear. You will hear the word or phrase twice. Then, listen to two sentences in which that word or phrase is used. (The second sentence is taken from the conversation you have heard.) Next, write down what you think that word or phrase means. Make an intelligent guess, using context clues.

1. Listen and write: _____
    Meaning:
2. Listen and write: _____
    Meaning:
3. Listen and write: _____
    Meaning:
4. Listen and write: _____
    Meaning:
5. Listen and write: _____
    Meaning:
6. Listen and write: _____
    Meaning:

Now that you have done the vocabulary in context, listen to the interview again.

The Interview

Tape: Part One, again—The second listening 1

Reconstruction

Working with a partner, comment on each of the following phrases that your heard in the interview. Give the context for the phrase and explain as fully as possible what the person was talking about.

1. cordless phone
2. Kentucky Fried Chicken
3. a surgeon
4. a general practitioner
5. emergency room
6. suicide—a bottle of aspirin
7. a mild heart attack
8. a massive coronary
9. a motorcycle—car collision
10. a lot of blood
11. shaking with exhaustion
12. a penguin
13. the soap
14. gech mish olsun (Turkish)

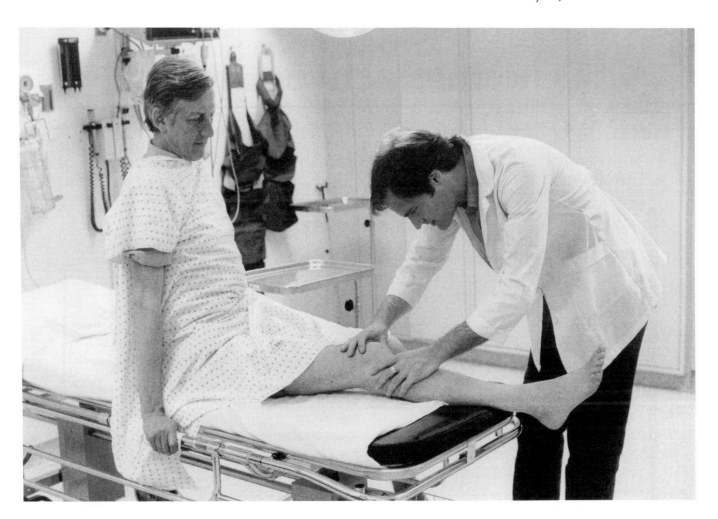

 # The Dialogue

 3

Tape: Part Three—Tom and Steve

Listen to this telephone conversation. Answer the following questions:

Questions

1. Who are the two speakers? What is their relationship?

2. What does Steve really want to do at this point?

3. What is Tom's advice to him?

4. Do you think that people at the age of seventeen or eighteen should know what they want to do professionally, or what kind of work they want to do?

The Interactive Listening

Tape: Part Four—Filling out a medical history 4

In this exercise you will listen to an inteview between Dr. Rose and Mrs. Gold, who is seeing the doctor for the first time. You are the doctor. On the form below, fill out information on Mrs. Gold.

Medical History

NAME _____ AGE _____

ADDRESS _____ HEIGHT _____

WEIGHT _____

Please check (✓) any of these
problems that you have had:

Frequent colds _____

Frequent sore throats _____

Frequent headaches _____

Allergies _____

Stomach problems _____

Kidney problems _____

High blood pressure _____

Anemia _____

Mental depression _____

Serious injuries _____

Heart condition _____

Please check (✓) any of these
diseases that you have had:

Chickenpox _____

Measles _____

Rubella _____

Mumps _____

Scarlet Fever _____

Polio _____

Whooping Cough _____

Tuberculosis _____

Diabetes _____

Hepatitis _____

Ulcers _____

Epilepsy _____

Are you taking any medications? _____

Which ones? _____

Are you allergic to any medications? _____

Which ones? _____

Have you had any operations? _____

Please describe them briefly and give the dates: _____

_____

_____

Have you ever been hospitalized for any other reason? _____

Please describe briefly and give the dates: _____

Does anyone have or has anyone in your family had:

	WHO	RELATION
Diabetes		
Cancer		
Heart condition		

Other information:

The Projects

A choice of communicative activities

Choose one of the following projects. You may work alone or with one or two classmates.

Project One

Develop a vocabulary lesson. Below is a list of medical specialties and beside each is the name of the specialist. Find out the meaning of each for your classmates. Add five more to the list and find out the meanings of those. Teach your classmates the meanings of those on the list as well as the ones you have added.

internal medicine	internist	oncology	oncologist
radiology	radiologist	plastic surgery	plastic surgeon
psychiatry	psychiatrist	dermatology	dermatologist
pathology	pathologist	_____	_____
geriatrics	geriatrician	_____	_____
anaesthesiology	anaesthetist	_____	_____
orthopedics	orthopedist	_____	_____
gastroenterology	gastroenterologist	_____	_____

Project Two

Take a poll. Below are some reasons for choosing a particular doctor. Add several more if you wish to. Ask 10 people to look at the list and choose the 5 that are most important to them. If they want to add something to the list, they may. Be prepared to tell the class what were the most important qualifications and determining factors.

1. the medical school she or he attended

2. the hospital she or he is associated with

3. his or her reputation

4. a referral from someone you trust

5. location

6. gender (male or female)

7. willingness to answer questions and explain

8. friendly, someone you can talk to

9. busy but not overbooked (returns calls, can see you when necessary)

10. his or her medical philosophy (cautious, operates quickly, attitude toward medication, etc.)

Project Three

If you know a doctor, interview him or her. Find out why the person became a doctor, how difficult it was, how the person chose his or her specialty, the advantages, the disadvantages. Report on your interview to the class.

Project Four

Read the following article. It is titled *My First Stab Wound*, and it appeared in the *Washington Post*. After you have read it, tell your class about it, comparing and contrasting the author's experiences in the emergency room with Tom Hyatt's. Prepare a vocabulary list of medical terms (e.g., catheter, vital signs) and distribute copies to your classmates explaining the meanings of the terms.

My First Stab Wound

A Pre-Dawn Emergency Initiates an Intern

By Rebecca Rich
Special to The Washington Post

Every doctor has certain firsts they remember. I remember very well the first patient I took care of as an intern—not a fascinating medical mystery, just my first patient. When I think about my short career as an emergency room physician, I especially think of my first stab wound.

If you are a surgical resident at a trauma center, at a big city hospital, stab and gunshot wounds are a dime a dozen. But our hospital, though urban, is smaller, and we're not a trauma center. Theoretically, this means we should see few trauma cases. Rescue [the rescue squad of paramedics who answer emergency calls] is supposed to take these patients (people who are shot, stabbed, burned, beaten badly, fall from a great height or are in serious car accidents) to regional trauma centers, and ambulances usually do.

When police are doing the transporting, though, they don't have

any life-support equipment so they often scoop these people into the back seat and get to the closest ER. Since our hospital is near both a big housing project with a lot of violence and a hot gathering spot for young people to get drunk, we see more trauma than I'd expected.

It was 5 a.m. and quiet. I was drawing blood on an asthmatic. The nurse (at night in our ER there's one doctor and one nurse, with in-house backup in all the specialties) had just headed to the bathroom. I can usually hear the sound of ambulances pulling up outside, and tonight I heard the beep-beep-beep of Rescue backing up. I glanced up, but since I had a needle in my asthmatic's arm I stayed put. The Rescue guys were bringing in the stretcher with more speed than usual, and one of them yelled, "It's a real one!" I ran over to the bed, where I saw a patient with two stab wounds, one to the chest, one to the abdomen. By then the nurse was at my side. The patient was unconscious, and we couldn't get a blood pressure, though he had a thready pulse in

ILLUSTRATION BY STEPHANIE SHEILDHOUSE FOR THE WASHINGTON POST

the big neck arteries we look for in emergencies. We needed more hands; this guy probably needed surgery right away. We threw on gloves and started CPR (cardiopulmonary resuscitation) and cutting off his clothes.

Every time the nurse pushed on his chest, blood would gush out the chest wound; the abdominal wound seemed to have stopped bleeding. We yelled toward the desk to call a "code" (announce an emergency on the overhead page); during the day the clerk would just dial the emergency phone and the ER would

94

suddenly swarm with people responding to the code. Now, at 5 a.m., the Rescue guys were the only ones at the desk, doing their paper work: they looked at us blankly. One of us continued CPR while the other one dialed the code. The nurse and I never really looked closely at the wounds; our patient's lack of an acceptable blood pressure was indication enough to us that he was seriously injured. In fact, we really worked around the wounds, covering them with clean dressings, attempting to tide this guy over with CPR until his wounds could be definitively fixed by the surgeons in the OR (operating room).

In less than a minute, our corner of the ER was filled with people. The respiratory therapists had taken over at the head of the bed, using an inflatable bag to provide artificial respiration (instead of mouth-to-mouth). Nurses and surgical residents were over the shoulders and arms, repeatedly taking blood pressure, drawing blood and placing big intravenous tubes into the arms and chest. The surgical intern was down at the groin, putting in a bladder catheter to monitor urine output. The anesthetists and OR nurses were hovering nearby getting ready for surgery, yelling at the blood bank to send blood down for transfusion—immediately. In the corridor, the police and detectives were starting to gather. And in the center of it all, the chief surgical resident had his arm in the chest wound doing an open heart massage. Within a few minutes of everyone's arrival, the patient in his bed was moving swiftly toward the elevators and the OR, with many tubes and staff attached, the chief surgical resident still in the center with his arm submerged.

What had been a mass of people around the stretcher just one minute ago was now an empty cubicle, the floor littered with blood and tubing and dressings and used equipment. What had been a din just a few minutes ago was now back to the usual pre-dawn quiet, except for the murmur of the detectives and excited chatter of the asthmatic and her companion about what had just gone on. It was only as we cleaned up the mess that we wondered: Who had stabbed him? Why? Did he have a job? A family?

We found out later that the patient had survived surgery; he had a laceration of the right ventricle of the heart, which was repaired, as well as damage to his spleen which was removed. He went to the intensive care unit where he did amazingly well, considering how badly hurt he had been, and subsequently was discharged. It seems as if a lot of the same people end up getting stabbed again; I hope this guy's stab wound—my first—is his last.

Rebecca Rich, a native of Washington, D.C., is an emergency room physician at Pennsylvania Hospital in Philadelphia. This is the first of an occasional series in which she describes her long days and nights in the ER.

Credit: Rebecca Rich, M.D.

Lesson 10: Connie Snow, building contractor

Introductory Reading

Connie Snow is an example of those people who surprise themselves when they make their vocational choice. She didn't make that choice until after she had graduated from college. "When I was a senior in college, if you had told me I was going to become a building contractor, I'd probably have said, 'You're crazy.'"

In college, Connie was an English major doing research on the music imagery in Shakespeare's plays. She thought she'd either write for a small town newspaper or teach English in a high school. But, she says, "After graduating from college I was working on a farm in California, and I discovered that I liked banging nails and doing nitty gritty building work."

But to be a successful contractor more is required than just enjoying being a good carpenter. The contractor needs to be a good organizer, both of time and of people. Connie says of herself, "I've always been an organizer. I like going out and lining up the people—the subcontractors and their trade skill crews—who need to be there tomorrow to do the plumbing or the wiring or the painting or heating or roofing . . . whatever.

"And also, I enjoy interfacing with many different people. In this job you're getting estimates from plumbers and you're down at city hall getting your building permits and lining up your framing inspection and insulation inspection. And getting your materials ordered—cuz if you don't order your windows in time, you're gonna get held up and everything else will get behind schedule so you lose a lot of time, and 'time is money.' Who is it that said that? Was it Benjamin Franklin?"

The contractor's main function, then, is to coordinate and manage a building project. But he or she also assumes responsibility for the completion of that project at a time and cost specified in the contract. So it is important that the contractor have a background in and/or a talent for not only some trade skill (plumbing, carpentry, electrical work, plastering, lathing . . .), but also time-management, people-management, and finance-management.

Job satisfaction? "Sure, there are satisfactions as a contractor," Connie says. "It is important to me to try to have people feel good about their work. I don't want us just to be building houses. I want us to do it right, and I want people to be excited about the job and to enjoy being there. It's really an idea about work. A fun and healthy work situation, that's what I want to help create. When that happens, that's the greatest satisfaction."

In the interview with Connie, she talks about a very special building project she is now managing. ✑

Work Related Vocabulary

These words or phrases are used in the interview you're about to hear. In groups discuss the vocabulary, sharing knowledge and using a dictionary when needed. Check (✓) off those words you already know. If a word or phrase is new to you and you want to learn it, in the space beside it either write its meaning in English or in your own language or write an English sentence using it.

1. a hammer and a saw
2. a contractor
3. speculation (in housing)
4. preplanning
5. a building site
6. mortgage money
7. a subcontractor
8. a low interest rate
9. a credit rating
10. monthly payments
11. a foundation (of a building)
12. framing (of a building)

Additional vocabulary

1. macho
2. to screen
3. eligible
4. disgruntled

 # The Interview

Tape: Part One—The first listening 1

Listen to the interview trying to get a general understanding, the gist, of what the discussion is about and then answer the following questions:

Questions

1. What did you learn about Connie and her work in this first listening?

2. What are the most interesting things you learned about Connie and her work?

3. Did anything you learned from the interview surprise you?

 # Vocabulary in Context

Tape: Part Two—Listening exercise 2

Listen to the recording and write down the word or phrase you hear. You will hear the word or phrase twice. Then, listen to two sentences in which that word or phrase is used. (The second sentence is taken from the conversation you have heard.) Next, write down what you think that word or phrase means. Make an intelligent guess, using context clues.

1. Listen and write: _____
    Meaning:

2. Listen and write: _____
    Meaning:

3. Listen and write: _____
    Meaning:

4. Listen and write: _____
    Meaning:

5. Listen and write: _____
    Meaning:

6. Listen and write: _____
    Meaning:

Now that you have done the vocabulary in context, listen to the interview again.

99

✳ The Interview

Reconstruction

Working with a partner comment on each of the following phrases that you heard in the interview. Give the context for the phrase and explain as fully as possible what the person was talking about.

1. a hammer and a saw

2. The Great American Dream

3. "... my son and his new wife ..."

4. screening

5. Farmer's Home Administration

6. $18,000

7. forty hours

8. ... cousins, brothers ...

9. 1% interest

10. the foundations

11. disgruntled and exhausted

 # The Dialogue

 3

Tape: Part Three—Connie and a young couple

Listen to this conversation. Answer the following questions:

Questions

1. What decision are Paula and John making?

2. What are the factors in their decision?

3. What do they finally decide? Why?

RANCH

One floor

26'0"

42'0"   20'0"

CLOS.

BATH

BEDROOM

CLOS.

Laundry   CLOS.

KITCHEN DINING

Sliding door

Storage

GARAGE

BEDROOM

CLOS.

BATH

DOWN

LIVING ROOM

CAPE

32'0"

Stove   Sink

BATH

Ref.   CLOS.

DINING AREA   KITCHEN

24'0"

DOWN

CLOS.

LIVING ROOM

CLOS.

UP

BEDROOM

CLOS.

First floor

Access door

CLOS.   CLOS.   CLOS.   CLOS.

DOWN

BATH

BEDROOM

BEDROOM

Second floor

SALT BOX

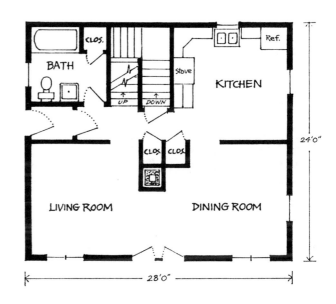

First floor

BATH

CLOS.

KITCHEN

Stove

Ref.

UP

DOWN

CLOS

CLOS

LIVING ROOM

DINING ROOM

24'0"

28'0"

Access door

Access door

CLOS.

CLOS.

DOWN

BEDROOM

BEDROOM

BEDROOM

CLOS.

Second floor

The Interactive Listening

4

Tape: Part Four—Listen, visualize and draw

In this exercise you are asked to visualize what you hear on the tape and then to finish the drawings below based on the descriptions given. You need not be a great artist, but have fun being creative in your interpretations.

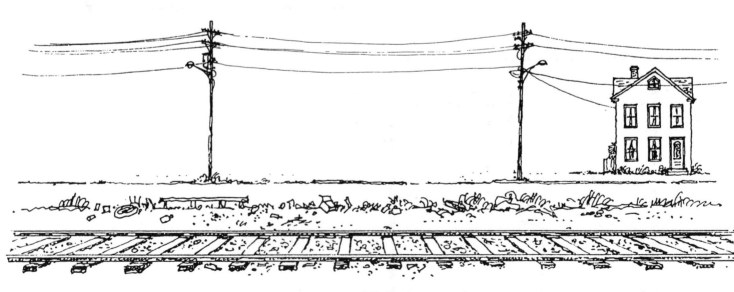

The Projects

A *choice of communicative activities*

Choose one of the following projects. You may work alone or with one or two classmates.

Project One

Study Connie's house plans on pages 102 & 103. Explain them to your class pointing out the differences and using lots of vocabulary. Describe one or more typical houses from your culture and explain how it or they compare with Connie's houses.

Project Two

Poll ten people on the following question. You add the final three options. Present your results.

You are about to have a three bedroom house built for you, your spouse, and your two children (or for another combination of four people). Although it is a basic house with two bathrooms and three bedrooms, you are able to choose three, and only three, luxury items that would make this a much more luxurious home. Read through the items and list three that you would choose.

1. *Central air conditioning*
2. *An additional bedroom for guests*
3. *An outdoor swimming pool*
4. *A garage (You now park in the driveway.)*
5. *A deck that you can sit out on, or even eat dinner on in the warm weather*
6. *A den (study, library)*
7. *Some additional land (for a large garden)*
8. *A family room with a built-in large screen TV*
9. *An extra full bathroom*
10. *A laundry with sink, washer, dryer, and room for ironing (otherwise this is in the kitchen)*
11. *A separate large dining room (This now is a small room adjoining the kitchen)*
12. *A lot of extra storage space*
13. _____
14. _____
15. _____

Project Three

Interview two men and two women about what they are able to do to build a home or to make repairs once they own a home. Can they do basic carpentry work? Can they paint well? Can they do electrical repairs and plumbing repairs? Can they put up shelves? etc. Prepare a list of questions ahead of time. Ask them where they learned to do the things they can do? (School? Father? Mother? etc.) Organize the results of the interviews and present the material to the class.

Project Four

Find out about the cost of the least expensive home you could buy where you are now living. What is the cost of an average home in this area. What is the cost of a very expensive home. To do this, speak to realtors and look at the advertisements in the newspaper. If you are from another country, compare these costs to the cost of homes in your country. At the same time compare incomes. In other words, what would make it possible for a family to buy one of these homes? How much income would they have to have? Present your findings to the class.

Project Five

Read and report on the following article. The article is about "Habitat for Humanity," an organization interested in providing affordable housing for low-income families. When you read it, you will be surprised by two of the people who helped to do manual labor. Read the article. Tell the class about it and also provide a good vocabulary list for your fellow classmates.

Habitat For Humanity

Although construction is the largest industry in the United States and home building is the largest category in it, in a booming real estate market there is almost no opportunity for the poor, the lower middle class, and, in some areas, even the middle class to own a dwelling of their own. This is a difficult situation to accept in a country where blue collar workers have always taken great pride in caring for and improving their own homes, yards, and gardens.

Although local, state, and federal government agencies have been involved in helping to provide low cost housing, the need has always surpassed the production. Some successful ventures in providing affordable housing have been undertaken by small grassroots organizations interested in helping people who cannot afford adequate shelter to build their own houses with as much volunteer labor and donated materials as possible. This tradition goes back to pioneer days when families and their neighbors got together to build log cabins for each other. At that time, a "house raising" was a joyous occasion and everyone, including young children, helped.

Today such a cooperative venture can still provide a happy family with a house of their own built at a minimum cost. As they do on a standard mortage, the family pays for the house over a fixed time period, but they usually do not pay interest and no one makes a profit. The new proud homeowners know that they, their families, and their friends have helped to build the house, and they feel tremendous pride in this "pioneer" accomplishment.

One organization that does this is **Habitat for Humanity,** an ecumenical, grassroots, Christian group dedicated to helping individuals, churches, companies, and foundations become partners with **Habitat** to help the poor change their living conditions. They do this in both the United States and in other countries such as Kenya and Peru.

Habitat projects include not only the building of new homes, but the rehabilitation of old buildings into pleasant, modern housing.

Since 1984, former President Jimmy Carter and his wife, Rosalynn, have been active supporters of **Habitat**, active in more than the sense of donating and raising money or making speeches on its behalf. This is how Rosalynn Carter describes one of her **Habitat** experiences in the Carters' book *Everything To Gain: Making the Most of the Rest of Your Life* (Random House, New York, 1987)—she was a volunteer in a rehabilitation project: "I was first assigned, along with two other women, to clean up the floor that still remained in one corner of the back section. We scraped up layers of old glue and paint and patches of linoleum that were stuck to it, removed nails that were sticking up, and had made it perfectly smooth when one of the men came over with a sheet of plywood and said, 'Nail it down.' Nail it down? Before we left home, I had told Jimmy that I would do anything but hammer. I didn't think I could use a hammer and I didn't want to use a hammer. We nailed it down! At first it took me fifteen or twenty strokes for each nail, but before the week was over I could drive one in with only four or five strokes!"

And Jimmy Carter tells us why they participate: "There is great satisfaction in being able to 'make a difference' for someone who needs help. The tiredness that comes from any physical activity is all worthwhile, and the spirit sometimes soars. Working with **Habitat** has been that kind of experience for us. Of all the activities we have undertaken since leaving the White House, it is certainly one of the most inspiring. To help build a home for people who have never lived in a decent place and never dreamed of owning a home of their own can bring both a lot of joy and an emotional response. One has only to have had the experience to know what it means—to the one who is giving time and energy and to the one who is receiving the new home."